T5-ALS-912

PRISMS

INSIGHTS INTO CHUMASH
BEREISHIS & THE YAMIM TOVIM

MICHAEL SCHOEN

TARGUM/FELDHEIM

First published 1990

ISBN 0-944070-53-1

Copyright © 1990 by Michael Schoen

All rights reserved

No part of this publication may be translated, reproduced, stored in a retrieval system or transmitted, in any form or by any means, electronic, mechanical, photocopying, recording or otherwise, without prior permission in writing from the publisher and copyright holder.

Phototypeset at Targum Press

Published by:
Targum Press Inc.
22700 W. Eleven Mile Rd.
Southfield, Mich. 48034

Distributed by:
Philipp Feldheim Inc.
200 Airport Executive Park
Spring Valley, N.Y. 10977

Distributed in Israel by:
Nof Books Ltd.
POB 23646
Jerusalem 91235

Printed in Israel

בס"ד

10 כסלו תש"ן

[handwritten letter in Hebrew]

ידידי הנעלה הרב מהור"ר ר' מיכאל שון שליט"א מוציא ספר רעיונות
ובאורים בדברי חז"ל על חומש בראשית ליום הזכרון של אמו החשובה ע"ה
שזה יהי לעלוי נשמתה. עיינתי בכמה מקומות בענינים שונים ומצאתי
שנאמרו בדעת נבונה ולב רגיש והדברים ערבים ללב ונעימים לאוזן ובודאי
זה יהי לעלוי נשמתה אבל לא רק זה הוא לעלוי נשמתה אלא כל עבודתו
והתעסקות של ידידי ר' מיכאל ללמוד התורה והתמסרותו הנפלאה להקים את
התורה ללמוד וללמד ולקרב בני ישראל לעבודת ד' ולתורתו הם עלוי
לנשמתה הק' ובראַ מזכי... ונזכה לראות בנחמת ציון וירושלים ושבו
בנים לגבולם בב"א
דב שורצמן

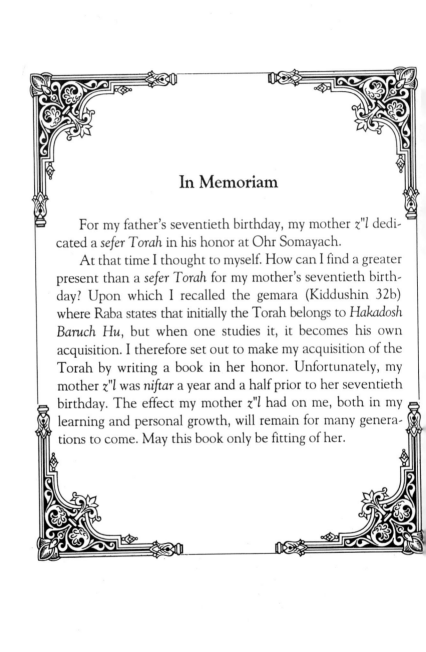

In Memoriam

For my father's seventieth birthday, my mother *z"l* dedicated a *sefer Torah* in his honor at Ohr Somayach.

At that time I thought to myself. How can I find a greater present than a *sefer Torah* for my mother's seventieth birthday? Upon which I recalled the gemara (Kiddushin 32b) where Raba states that initially the Torah belongs to *Hakadosh Baruch Hu*, but when one studies it, it becomes his own acquisition. I therefore set out to make my acquisition of the Torah by writing a book in her honor. Unfortunately, my mother *z"l* was *niftar* a year and a half prior to her seventieth birthday. The effect my mother *z"l* had on me, both in my learning and personal growth, will remain for many generations to come. May this book only be fitting of her.

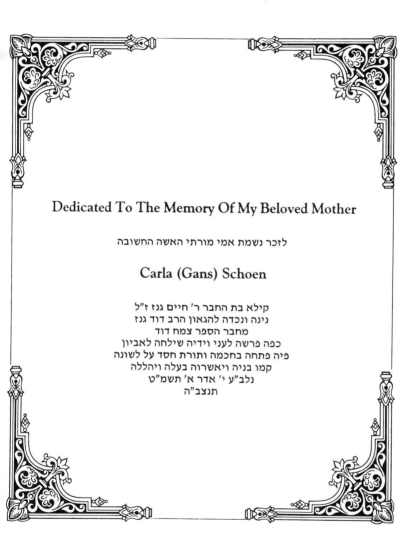

Dedicated To The Memory Of My Beloved Mother

לזכר נשמת אמי מורתי האשה החשובה

Carla (Gans) Schoen

קילא בת החבר ר' חיים גנז ז"ל
נינה ונכדה להגאון הרב דוד גנז
מחבר הספר צמח דוד
כפה פרשה לעני וידיה שילחה לאביון
פיה פתחה בחכמה ותורת חסד על לשונה
קמו בניה ויאשרוה בעלה ויהללה
נלב"ע י' אדר א' תשמ"ט
תנצב"ה

Acknowledgments

There are many people who have had an effect upon my life who should be acknowledged, but that would be a book in its own right. So I've limited my acknowledgments to those who helped me with this book and a few others who without doubt were the pillars of my growth.

To Helena Emmett for typing the original manuscript. To the entire staff of Targum Press for their suggestions and many hard hours of work to meet the deadline. To Feldheim Publishers for concluding the final stages of the publishing and distribution of the book. To Rabbi Mendel Weinbach for looking over the material and offering his suggestions.

To Ohr Somayach Institutions, where I gave classes in Chumash for many years, upon which the essence of this book was formulated.

To my father, may he live to one hundred and twenty, who has consistently supported and guided me so that I could devote my life to learning, teaching, and building Torah. May my dear father and his newly married wife, Margaret, only merit *simchas* and much *nachas* from their children and grandchildren.

To all my children, for their encouragement and patience while I was occupied in the writing of this book.

And last but not least to my dear wife, Miriam, to whom one can apply the words of Rabbi Akivah: Everything I've attained is due to her—שלי ושלכם שלה—May we merit together to bring up all our children in the proper way.

Table of Contents

כי נר מצוה ותורה אור...

For a mitzvah is a candle and Torah is light...
(Mishlei 6:23)

The Torah is compared to light. Just as light, monochrome at first glance, bursts into multi-hued magnificence when focused through a prism, so, too, is the Torah: At first glance only one interpretation can be seen, but as one delves into it, many more explanations appear. For this reason I have chosen "Prisms" as the title of this book. I only pray that the interpretations I have suggested should be one of the "seventy facets of the Torah."

CHUMASH BEREISHIS

בראשית
Bereishis

בראשית ברא אלקים...

In the beginning, God created...

(Bereishis 1:1)

אמר רב יצחק לא היה צריך להתחיל את התורה אלא
מהחודש הזה לכם שהיא מצוה ראשונה שנצטוו בה
ישראל ומה טעם פתח בבראשית משום (תהילים קי"א)
כח מעשיו הגיד לעמו לתת להם נחלת גוים שאם
יאמרו אומות העולם לישראל לסטים אתם שכבשתם
ארצות שבעה גוים הם אומרים להם כל הארץ של
הקב"ה היא הוא בראה ונתנה לאשר ישר בעיניו
ברצונו נתנה להם וברצונו נטלה מהם ונתנה לנו.
(רש"י ד"ה בראשית)

R. Yitzchak said: The Torah ought to have begun with
"This month is for you," the first mitzvah that Yisrael
was commanded... What is the reason it opened with
"In the beginning"? Because "He has told the people of
the power of His works, that He may give them the
inheritance of the nations" (Tehillim 111:6). If the
nations of the world will tell Yisrael, "You are thieves,
for you stole the land of the seven nations," they can
say to them, "All the land belongs to the Holy One,
blessed be He; He created it and gave it to whomever

He wished. In His desire, He gave to them; in His desire
He took it from them and gave it to us."

(Rashi, ad loc.)

וקשה ומה בכך אם יאמרו לסטים אתם וכי בעבור זה
ישנה סדר התורה?

(כלי יקר בראשית א:א)

This is difficult: And what if they would say, "You are
thieves"? Would the Torah change its order just for this?

(Kli Yakar, Bereishis 1:1)

Rashi states that the reason the Torah begins with the world's
creation and not with the first commandment of sanctifying the
new moon is so the other nations would not have a claim against
the Jewish people for conquering Eretz Yisrael. God, who created
the world, can give it to anyone whom He chooses.

The Kli Yakar asks: Is it so important that nations know
we have a right to Eretz Yisrael? Is this a reason to refrain
from beginning the Torah with the first commandment, as
seems more natural?

(ספרי) אף לאחר שתגלו היו מצוייינים במצות הניחו
תפילין עשו מזוזות כדי שלא יהיו לכם חדשים כשתחזרו
וכן הוא אומר (ירמיה לא) הציבי לך ציונים.

(רש"י דברים יא:יח ד"ה ושמתם את דברי)

(Sifri) Even after you are exiled be careful with mitzvos—put on tefillin, place mezuzos—so that they [the
mitzvos] should not be new to you when you return, as
it states, "Set up signposts for yourself" (Yirmiyahu 31:20).

(Rashi, Devarim 11:18)

Here, Rashi states that the reason the Jews kept the
commandments outside of Eretz Yisrael was so that when
they returned, it wouldn't feel as if the mitzvos were new. It
appears from this Rashi that the total fulfillment of all mitzvos can be reached only in Eretz Yisrael.

Since the ultimate fulfillment of the mitzvos can only be

reached in Eretz Yisrael, it follows that the Torah should belong to the nation that has the right to Eretz Yisrael. Therefore, before the Torah could begin discussing the various commandments, it had to deal with ownership of the land. Since Eretz Yisrael belongs to the Jewish people, the Torah does as well.

* * *

ויאמר אלקים יהי מארת ברקיע השמים להבדיל בין
היום ובין הלילה והיו לאתת ולמועדים ולימים ושנים.

God said: "Let there be lights in the firmament of heaven, to divide between the day and the night; and they will be for signs and for seasons, for days and for years."

(Bereishis 1:14)

פ' אחר לאותות אלו שבתות שנאמר והיה לאות
ביני וכו'. ולמועדים אלו שלש רגלים. ולימים אלו
ראשי חדשים כמו חדש ימים. ושנים אלו ראשי השנים...
והבן שלא חשב יום הכפורים מפני שעשרת ימים שבין כסא
לעשור נקראים ראש השנה לפי ששנות החמה יתרים על
שנת הלבנה כמספרם ולכן המעשים הנאותים הנפעלים
בימים אלו חשובים ככל השנה.

(אדרת אליהו פרק א:יד)

Another explanation: for signs—these are Sabbaths, as it says, "It shall be a sign between Me"; for seasons—these are the three pilgrimage festivals; for days—these are the new moons, as in "thirty days" [Bereishis 29:14]; and years— these are new years...Understand that Yom Kippur was not referred to because the ten days between the throne [Rosh Hashanah] and the tenth [Yom Kippur] are called Rosh Hashanah since the solar year is greater than the lunar year by their number, and thus the proper deeds done in these days are considered as the entire year.

(Aderes Eliyahu 1:14)

The Vilna Gaon associates the time difference between the lunar and the solar year with the Ten Days of Repentance. But what is the connection between the two?

בראשית ברא אלקים את השמים ואת הארץ.

In the beginning, God created the heaven and the earth.
(Bereishis 1:1)

ולא אמר ברא ד' שבתחלה עלה במחשבה לבראותו
במדת הדין וראה שאין העולם מתקיים והקדים מדת
רחמים ושתפה למדת הדין והיינו דכתיב ביום עשות
ד' אלקים ארץ ושמים.
(רש"י ד"ה ברא אלוקים)

It does not say "the Lord created," for in the beginning He
planned to create it with the trait of strict justice. He saw
that the world could not exist, and so He brought forth the
trait of mercy to join the trait of strict justice, as it says, "on
the day the Lord, God, created the earth and the heaven."
(Rashi, ad loc.)

What was it that God saw that made Him decide to
create the world with the trait of mercy as well as justice?

ויעש אלקים את שני המארת הגדלים את המאור
הגדל לממשלת היום ואת המאור הקטן לממשלת הלילה
ואת הכוכבים.

*God made the two great lights; the great light to rule the day,
and the small light to rule the night; and the stars.*
(Bereishis 1:16)

שוים נבראו ונתמעטה הלבנה על שקטרגה ואמרה אי
אפשר לשני מלכים שישתמשו בכתר אחד.
(רש"י ד"ה המאורות הגדולים)

They were created equal, and the moon was diminished
because she complained and said: "It is impossible for
two kings to share one crown."
(Rashi, ad loc.)

מיום ראשון נבראו וברביעי צוה עליהם להתלות ברקיע
וכן כל תולדות שמים וארץ נבראו ביום ראשון וכל אחד

ואחד נקבע ביום שנגזר עליו הוא שכתוב את השמים
לרבות תולדותיהם ואת הארץ לרבות תולדותיהם.
(רש"י בראשית א:יד ד"ה יהי מארת וגו')

They were created from the first day, and on the fourth it was commanded to hang them in the firmament; and thus it was for all of heaven and earth. They were created on the first day, and set up on the day decreed. This is why it states [in Bereishis 1:1] "the heaven"—to include its results—"and the earth"—to include its results.

(Rashi, Bereishis 1:14)

On the first day of creation, when, according to Rashi, the moon was created, the moon, in its haughtiness, requested to be made larger than the sun. For the first time ever Hashem implemented the trait of strict justice by making the moon smaller. When Hashem saw that the physical creation could so drastically change through His judgment, He realized that the world could not exist with strict justice alone. The moon, as the first object which incurred strict judgment, stands for this trait.

מעולם לא ראתה חמה פגימתה של לבנה...דחלשה דעתה.

The sun never saw the missing portion of the moon...so that she [the moon] should not feel humiliated.

(Rosh Hashanah 23b)

Hashem made the sun incapable of seeing the moon's fate in order not to shame it. With this action, God first implemented the trait of mercy in the world; thus, the sun became the symbol of that trait.

One can suggest that the implementation of the trait of mercy actually took place on the first Shabbos of creation. For then the creation process ceased and the world began to function as we know it today. Only then did the sun and moon move in their orbits in such a way that the sun could not see what the moon lacked.

ויכל אלקים ביום השביעי מלאכתו אשר עשה וישבת
ביום השביעי מכל מלאכתו אשר עשה.

On the seventh day God ended the work He had done; He rested on the seventh day from all the work He had done.

(Bereishis 2:2)

...ד"א מה היה העולם חסר מנוחה באת שבת באת
מנוחה כלתה ונגמרה המלאכה.
(רש"י ד"ה ויכל אלקים ביום השביעי)

...Another explanation: What was the world missing? Rest. Came Shabbos, came rest, and the work was finished and ended.

(Rashi, ad loc.)

This raises an obvious question: What kind of creation is rest? Doesn't "rest" show a lack of something, a refraining from action? How can something negative be created?

Bearing in mind that the trait of mercy came into existence on Shabbos, the answer becomes clear. On that first Shabbos there was "rest"—rest from the trait of strict justice. The trait of mercy had been created!

Rosh Hashanah, the Day of Judgment, is the time of strict justice. In our prayers, we remember the Patriarch Yitzchak, who stands for judgment. Yom Kippur, though, is the time of mercy, the ultimate application of "seek the Lord where He can be found, call Him when He is near" (Yeshayahu 55:6).

The day of Yom Kippur itself is an atonement, an indication of God's pure mercy.

Yom Kippur, as the day of pure mercy, is termed Shabbos Shabboson, an allusion to that first Shabbos when the trait of mercy was created.

Now the Vilna Gaon's association becomes very clear. The difference between the lunar year, symbolizing judgment, and the solar year, standing for mercy, is seen in the days between Rosh Hashanah, the Day of Judgment, and Yom Kippur, the day of pure mercy.

Noach

ויבא נח ובניו ואשתו ונשי בניו אתו אל התבה מפני מי
המבול.

*And Noach, along with his sons, his wife, and his sons'
wives, came onto the ark before the waters of the Flood.*

(Bereishis 7:7)

האנשים לבד והנשים לבד לפי שנאסרו בתשמיש
המטה מפני שהעולם שרוי בצער.

(רש"י ד"ה נח ובניו)

The men separately and the women separately, as marital relations were forbidden because the world was en-
veloped in suffering.

(Rashi, ad loc.)

From the wording of the *posuk*, with the men being listed
separately from the women, Rashi learns that marital relations were prohibited in the ark.

צא מן התבה אתה ואשתך ובניך ונשי בניך אתך.

*Leave the ark, you and your wife and your sons and your
sons' wives along with you.*

(Bereishis 8:16)

איש ואשתו כאן התיר להם תשמיש המטה.
(רש"י ד"ה אתה ואשתך)

> Man and wife: Here He permitted marital relations.
> (Rashi, ad loc.)

Since the verse now mentions them in pairs, Rashi deduces that at this point, when leaving the ark, marital relations became permitted.

However, the verse later continues, "And Noach went out, along with his sons, and his wife, and his sons' wives" (Bereishis 8:18). The Kli Yakar points out that the men are listed separately from the women, not as pairs. Noach did not listen to God and refrained from marital relations.

Later, God commands: "Be fruitful and multiply, swarm in the earth and multiply within it" (Bereishis 9:7). Here Rashi explains: "…The first [occasion these words appeared was] as a blessing; now as a command."

Three questions can be raised here. First, why did Noach not heed God's admonition to resume marital relations? Second, why were relations first permitted as an option and later given as a command? Third, why did God make a covenant with Noach not to destroy the world again? Was it not possible that the people might once again come to sin as Noach's generation had?

The Kli Yakar comments:

> אע"פ שהתיר הקב"ה לנח תשמיש מ"מ לא קבל
> עליו כי אמר פן יוסיפו לחטוא ויבואו מי המבול
> וישטפום ולמה זה יוליד לריק ולבהלה עד אשר
> נשבע ד' שלא להביא עוד מי המבול אז נאמר
> פרו ורבו וגו'.

> Although the Holy One, blessed be He, permitted relations to Noach, nevertheless, he did not take it upon himself, for he said: "Perhaps they [my offspring] will continue to sin, and the flood waters will drown them. Why should they be born for nought and destruction?"

God swore not to bring another flood, and then it was
said: Be fruitful and multiply, etc.

(Kli Yakar, Bereishis 8:16)

This approach answers the first question of why Noach
did not resume marital relations. The Flood came upon the
world because of the sin of stealing, as Rashi clearly points
out: "Their decree was sealed only because of stealing" (Rashi,
Bereishis 6:13).

A person steals because he feels that everything belongs
to him. When Noach came out of the ark, he and his family
were the only remaining people on earth, and it was natural
that they should feel that everything belonged to them. Yet
Noach's first action was to sacrifice his animals to God:

ויבן נח מזבח לד' ויקח מכל הבהמה הטהורה
ומכל העוף הטהור ויעל עלת במזבח.

*And Noach built an altar to God, and took from each pure
animal and each pure bird, and brought burnt-offerings
upon the altar.*

(Bereishis 8:20)

By his action, Noach showed that God, and not he, was
the true owner of the earth. With this, Noach atoned for the
sin of stealing. At this point God was willing to make the
covenant with Noach not to bring another flood; thus He
could change His permission to be fruitful to a command, for
Noach no longer feared the destruction of his offspring.

Lech Lecha

ויאמר ד' אל אברם לך לך מארצך וממולדתך ומבית
אביך אל הארץ אשר אראך.

*God said to Avram: "Go, you, from your land and from
your birthplace and from your father's home to the land that
I will show you."*

(Bereishis 12:1)

The Kli Yakar asks why God used the three expressions:
your land, your birthplace, your father's home.

At the same time, Rashi explains *"lech lecha"* (go, you) to
mean that Avraham should go for his own pleasure and his
own benefit. Why does God have to emphasize that this
journey to Eretz Yisrael is for Avraham's benefit? Must not
Avraham heed God even if the journey isn't for his good?

These words may hold a message for all generations about
coming to Eretz Yisrael. There are three reasons why a person
might not want to come to Eretz Yisrael. First, he may feel an
attachment to his homeland—"your land." Second, a person
often fears change—"your birthplace"—the way things have been
from the very beginning. Third, a person has family attach-
ments—"your father's home." Says God: All these reasons are

not acceptable to decline coming to Eretz Yisrael. However, the journey must be "for your benefit" as a Jew. If this is not so, a person has a legitimate reason not to come to Eretz Yisrael.

*   *   *

אמרי נא אחתי את למען ייטב לי בעבורך וחיתה
נפשי בגללך.

Please say you are my sister so that they will be good to me for your sake, and because of you my life will be spared.
(Bereishis 12:13)

Rashi explains the words "so that they will be good to me" as "they will give me gifts," thus indicating that when Avraham entered Egypt he was concerned about receiving gifts. Can the very same man who later states that he shall not take "from a thread to a shoelace from all that is yours, [for] you shall not say, 'I made Avram wealthy' " (Bereishis 14:23) mention the gifts before his very life!

Before tackling this apparent contradiction, let us examine still another problematic issue. The Torah tells us that Sarah afflicted Hagar, as it states:

...ותענה שרי ותברח מפניה.

...Sarai was harsh with her, and she ran away from her.
(Bereishis 16:6)

Later, when the angel tried to convince Hagar to return to Sarah, he said:

...שובי אל גברתך והתעני תחת ידיה.

...Return to your mistress, and submit yourself to her.
(Bereishis 16:9)

Telling Hagar to go back and let Sarah afflict her does

not seem to be much of a reason for her to return!

All these problems can be solved by closely examining the motivations of Sarah and Avraham. Avraham and Sarah had one main purpose in life—to reveal God's presence to the entire world. They knew that only if they would be in a position of respect, if people would feel either subjected or indebted to them, would their arguments be given credence.

Avraham wanted to be given gifts upon his arrival in Egypt so that all would see that he was a man to be honored; later he would be more able to influence them. However, when the five kings offered Avraham gifts for saving their family and goods, they did so because they didn't want to feel indebted to him; they wanted to pay him off. To this, Avraham responds that he will take nothing.

This also explains Sarah's afflicting Hagar. If Hagar came under Sarah's authority, Sarah would then be better able to convince her of God's imminence. This is what the angel told Hagar: Your purpose is to go and afflict yourself under Sarah so that you will accept the idea of God's presence; therefore, return to your mistress.

The actions of Avraham and Sarah were not done for purposes of self-aggrandizement; their only motivation was the glory of God.

*   *   *

ולא נשא אתם הארץ לשבת יחדו כי היה רכושם רב
ולא יכלו לשבת יחדו.

And the land was not able to support them [Avraham and Lot] living together; for their wealth was great, that they could not dwell together.

(Bereishis 13:6)

Why is this idea repeated twice? There were two reasons that Avraham was unable to live with Lot. First, physically, the land could not hold both of them—"the land was not able to support them." Second, their different levels in spirituality and fear of God made it impossible for them to be together. This is what is alluded to in "they could not dwell together."

*   *   *

ויאמר אליו אני ד' אשר הוצאתיך מאור כשדים
לתת לך את הארץ הזאת לרשתה. ויאמר ד' אלקים
במה אדע כי אירשנה.

He said to him: "I am God who took you out of Ur Kasdim to give you this land to inherit." He said: "Lord, my God, with what shall I know that I will inherit?"

(Bereishis 15:7-8)

When Avraham asks God for an actual sign that he will inherit the land, God answers him with the covenant known as the *bris bein habesarim.*

The Ramban is puzzled by Avraham's question. Why did he ask for a covenant as a guarantee of receiving Eretz Yisrael? Surely Avraham did not question God's promise to him!

Later in the *parshah*, in the section on Avraham's circumcision, the verse states:

ואתנה בריתי ביני ובינך וארבה אותך במאד מאד.

I will make My covenant between Me and you, and I will greatly increase your numbers.

(Bereishis 17:2)

Rashi comments on this:

ברית של אהבה וברית הארץ להורישה לך ע"י מצוה זו.
(רש"י ד"ה ואתנה בריתי)

A covenant of love, and a covenant on the land, to hand it to you through this mitzvah.

(Rashi, ad loc.)

Rashi understands circumcision as yet another covenant for the receiving of Eretz Yisrael. Why is the second covenant necessary? Was not the *bris bein habesarim* sufficient?

The Ramban solves the problem he'd raised about why Avraham questioned God on His promise by explaining that Avraham was worried that the promise of Eretz Yisrael was contingent upon his descendants' fulfillment of the mitzvos. What Avraham sought was a guarantee that, no matter what, his children would receive the land.

This explanation, however, is difficult to understand. What right did Avraham have to make such a request? Why should his seed receive Eretz Yisrael if they didn't perform the mitzvos?

Perhaps this can be explained in the following manner. Avraham realized that if the Jewish people were to be considered like any other nation, by logic they should inherit Eretz Yisrael only if they fulfill the mitzvos and deserve it. What Avraham wanted was to make the Jews inherently different, so that they should be entitled to the land even if they didn't fulfill the mitzvos. God agrees, and in His first covenant, the *bris bein habesarim*, promises to make them different. Afterwards, God commands the circumcision—the first difference which separates the Jews from the other nations. How beautiful are Rashi's words now—through this mitzvah, this difference, the Jewish people will inherit their land.

Perhaps this is the meaning of the blessing recited at every *bris*:

כשם שנכנס לברית כן יכנס לתורה ולחפה ולמעשים
טובים.

Just as he entered [the covenant of] the *bris*, may he enter into Torah, *chuppah*, and good deeds.

The connection between circumcision and the other milestones are that all four represent the differences between the Jews and other nations.

At the giving of the Torah, the verse states: "And you shall be a treasure to Me from among all the nations... You will be for Me a kingdom of priests, a holy nation" (Shemos 19:5-6). It is the Torah which makes us God's special treasure.

Chuppah, too, exists only among the Jewish people: Only *Am Yisrael* can reach the completeness which one achieves through Jewish marriage (*nisuin*). Finally, good deeds are rooted in the characteristic of lovingkindness. Says the Rambam:

אסור לאדם להיות אכזרי ולא יתפייס אלא יהא
נוח לרצות וקשה לכעוס...וזהו דרכם של זרע
ישראל...אבל העובדי כוכבים...אינן כן.

> It is forbidden for a man to be cruel and not appeased; rather, he should be easily forgiving and difficult to anger...and this is the way of the seed of Yisrael...but the pagans...are not so.
>
> (Rambam, *Hilchos Teshuvah* 2:10)

The Rambam declares that certain aspects of lovingkindness are inherent traits possessed only by the seed of Yisrael.

The blessing at the *bris milah* is that just as the child merited the first difference of circumcision, so he should merit the other three differences of Torah, *chuppah*, and the lovingkindness that will bring on good deeds.

This blessing can be explained in still another manner. These accomplishments—*bris*, Torah, *chuppah*, and good deeds—share an important aspect: achieving them is not totally dependent upon the person.

In the case of circumcision, the child, obviously, is not circumcised willingly.

Of Torah, the Gemara says:

ואמר ר' יצחק אם יאמר לך אדם יגעתי ולא
מצאתי אל תאמן לא יגעתי ומצאתי אל תאמן יגעתי
ומצאתי תאמן הני מילי בדברי תורה אבל במשא ומתן
סייעתא הוא מן שמיא ולדברי תורה לא אמרן אלא
לחדודי אבל לאוקמי גירסא סייעתא מן שמיא היא.

R. Yitzchak said: If a person says to you I have toiled
and not found, do not believe; I did not toil and did
find, do not believe; I toiled and I found—believe.
When does this apply? In the words of Torah. But
business is with the help of Heaven. And in the matter
of Torah, this refers to sharpness only; but for *l'aukmei
girsa* [establishing the text] it is help from Heaven.

(*Megillah* 6b)

Rashi explains that *l'aukmei girsa* refers to remembering
the text of Torah. The most important part of Torah study is
dependent upon a gift from God.

In connection with *chuppah*, the Gemara says:

אמר רב יהודה אמר רב ארבעים יום קודם יצירת
הולד בת קול יוצאת ואומרת בת פלוני לפלוני.

Rav Yehudah said, Rav said: Forty days before the creation of the embryo, a heavenly voice goes out and says:
the daughter of this one [shall marry] this one...

(*Sotah* 2a)

One's partner in marriage is decided before birth by God.
Again, this milestone has nothing to do with the individual's
efforts.

Finally, the Gemara states:

דדרש רבה מאי דכתיב ויהיו מוכשלים לפניך בעת אפך
עשה בהם אמר ירמיה לפני הקב"ה רבונו של עולם
אפילו בשעה שכופין את יצרן ומבקשין לעשות צדקה
לפניך הכשילם בבני אדם שאינן מהוגנין כדי שלא
יקבלו עליהן שכר.

> Rabba interpreted: What is meant by "Let them stumble before You; in the time of Your wrath do so to them"? Yirmiyahu said to the Holy One, blessed be He: "Master of the World, even at the time that they bend their wills and seek to give charity before You, cause them to err [by giving to] men who are unworthy, so that they do not receive their reward [for their charity]."
>
> (*Bava Basra* 9b)

The Gemara declares that even in the realm of charity one needs the help of God to ensure that one gives to deserving recipients!

The blessing at a *bris* implies that just as this child was circumcised independent of his own efforts, so he should merit good fortune in these other milestones that similarly have nothing to do with his efforts: Torah, *chuppah*, and good deeds.

Finally, still another similarity exists among these four events: each help a person reach *shleimus*, perfection, through giving. The perfection achieved in circumcision is by removing (i.e., giving up) the *orlah* (foreskin). Interestingly, the word *shleimus* itself comes from the root *shalem*, to pay.

This is our blessing to the new infant: Just as a child achieves *shleimus* by giving up the foreskin, so may he achieve the perfection of Torah, whose most vital aspect is teaching, giving over, to others; *chuppah*, in which he gives of himself to his spouse; and good deeds, whose entire essence lies in giving to others.

Vayera

יקח נא מעט מים ורחצו רגליכם והשענו תחת העץ.

Let a little water be fetched, and wash your feet, and rest beneath the tree.

(Bereishis 18:4)

ע"י שליח והקב"ה שלם לבניו ע"י שליח שנאמר וירם משה את ידו ויך את הסלע.
(רש"י ד"ה יקח נא)

By means of a messenger; and the Holy One, blessed be He, repaid his children by means of a messenger, as it says: Moshe lifted his hand and struck the rock.

(Rashi, ad loc.)

Rashi explains that because Avraham did not present the water to his guests, the angels, himself, but gave it through a messenger, later God punished the Jewish people by giving them water through a messenger, Moshe.

Since Avraham himself did give them the bread, one may ask the question: Why did Avraham feel that only the bread must be presented personally?

In *Parshas Lech Lecha* I explained that Avraham's purpose was to teach all the other nations of the existence of one God. He did this by putting himself in a situation where he would be respected and other people would feel obligated to him.

Avraham thought that the angels were Arabs, as Rashi comments: "For he was certain that they were Arabs who worshiped the dust of their feet" (Rashi, Bereishis 18:4).

Avraham wanted these "Arabs" to feel obligated to him so that he could influence them. How appropriate then that he chose to present bread personally—for bread is the essence of man's existence. "I will take a morsel of bread, and you will comfort your hearts" (Bereishis 18:5). Offering that which is absolutely necessary for survival causes one to feel both subjugated and grateful.

Though drinking water, too, is essential to life, the water presented here was not for drinking but for washing only, as clearly stated in the verse.

חיי שרה

Chayei Sarah

ד׳ אלקי השמים אשר לקחני מבית אבי ומארץ מולדתי
ואשר דבר לי ואשר נשבע לי לאמר לזרעך אתן את
הארץ הזאת הוא ישלח מלאכו לפניך ולקחת אשה
לבני משם.

*God, the Lord of Heaven, who took me from my father's
house and from my native land, and who spoke with me and
swore to me: "I shall give this land to your offspring"; He
will send His angel before you and you will take a wife for
my son from there.*

(Bereishis 24:7)

Avraham's charge to Eliezer, and Eliezer's subsequent
interchanges with Rivkah, can raise several questions. Rashi
comments that the oath is referring back to the *bris bein
habesarim.* Yet what connection does this *bris* have with Avraham's confidence that Eliezer will find a suitable wife for
Yitzchak from among his own family?

והיה הנער אשר אמר אליה הטי נא כדך ואשתה
ואמרה שתה וגם גמליך אשקה אתה הכחת לעבדך
ליצחק ובה אדע כי עשית חסד עם אדני.

The girl to whom I say, "Please take down your pitcher and I will drink," and who will say, "Drink, and I will also water your camels," she, You will have appointed for Your servant, for Yitzchak. With this I shall know that You have shown kindness to my master.

(Bereishis 24:14)

רְאוּיָה הִיא לוֹ שֶׁתְּהֵא גּוֹמֶלֶת חֲסָדִים וּכְדַאי לִיכָּנֵס
בְּבֵיתוֹ שֶׁל אַבְרָהָם.
(רש"י ד"ה אתה הכחת)

She is worthy of him, for she will be kind and suitable to enter Avraham's household.

(Rashi ad loc.)

Only a girl who had the characteristic of lovingkindness could marry Yitzchak. Yet aren't there other characteristics to look for in a wife—modesty, sincerity, fear of God, and others? Why did Avraham insist on a *"gomeles chesed"* for his son?

וַיֹּאמֶר אֵלַי ד' אֲשֶׁר הִתְהַלַּכְתִּי לְפָנָיו יִשְׁלַח מַלְאָכוֹ אִתָּךְ
וְהִצְלִיחַ דַּרְכֶּךָ וְלָקַחְתָּ אִשָּׁה לִבְנִי מִמִּשְׁפַּחְתִּי וּמִבֵּית אָבִי.

He said to me, "God, before whom I walked, will send His angel with you, and give you success, and you will take a wife for my son from among my family and from my father's home."

(Bereishis 24:40)

When Eliezer repeats the interchange between himself and Avraham, he changes Avraham's words. Instead of quoting Avraham, who said that God who promised to give Eretz Yisrael to his offspring will find a wife for Yitzchak, he quotes Avraham as saying, "The God before whom I've walked will find a wife for my son." Why the change?

In *Parshas Lech Lecha* we explained that the *bris bein habesarim* was a covenant to make *Am Yisrael* inherently different from all other nations, so that they would be entitled to Eretz Yisrael even if they did not fulfill the commandments. If so, says Avraham to Eliezer, since in this *bris* God promised to make the characteristics of *Am Yisrael* different, God will have to find a woman who has these innate differences to create *Am Yisrael*, differences given only to members of the family of Avraham.

This explains why Avraham specifically sought a woman who was invested with lovingkindness, the characteristic that separates *Am Yisrael* from the other nations. As I explained in *Parshas Lech Lecha*, the Rambam clearly learns that there is an aspect of lovingkindness characteristic only of *Am Yisrael*.

Eliezer, however, didn't understand the promise of the *bris bein habesarim* in this fashion. He thought that Avraham's seed was entitled to Eretz Yisrael only if they fulfilled the commandments. For this reason he connects the guarantee of finding a suitable wife for Yitzchak to the fact that Avraham walked with God. He did not connect the *shidduch* with the promise of the *bris bein habesarim*. This is indicated by Eliezer's belief that there was a possibility of *Am Yisrael* descending from his daughter's offspring, as Rashi comments:

...בת היתה לו לאליעזר והיה מחזר למצוא עילה
שיאמר לו אברהם לפנות אליו להשיאו בתו אמר
לו אברהם בני ברוך ואתה ארור ואין ארור מדבק
בברוך.
(רש"י בראשית כד:לט ד"ה אלי לא תלך האשה)

> ... Eliezer had a daughter, and he was seeking the pretense that Avraham would tell him to turn to him and give him his daughter to wed [for Yitzchak]. Avraham said to him, "My son is blessed and you are cursed, and one who is cursed does not cleave to one who is blessed."
> (Rashi, Bereishis 24:39)

How beautiful was Avraham's reply—my son is blessed and you are cursed. *Am Yisrael* must be built from those who are inherently blessed—the family of Avraham.

תולדת

Toldos

גור בארץ הזאת ואהיה עמך ואברכך כי לך ולזרעך
אתן את כל הארצת האל והקמתי את השבעה אשר
נשבעתי לאברהם אביך. והרביתי את זרעך ככוכבי
השמים ונתתי לזרעך את כל הארצת האל והתברכו
בזרעך כל גויי הארץ. עקב אשר שמע אברהם בקלי
וישמר משמרתי מצותי חקותי ותורתי.

Live in this land and I will be with you, and bless you, for I will
give all of these lands to you and your descendants. I will fulfill
the oath that I swore to your father, Avraham. I will increase
your seed as the stars of the heaven, and give to your descendants
all of these lands, and all the nations of the land will be blessed in
your seed, because Avraham heeded My voice, and kept My
charge, My commandments, My statutes, and My Torah.
(Bereishis 26:3-5)

God connects giving Eretz Yisrael to Yitzchak's descendants,
and Yitzchak's own descendants' fruitfulness, to the fact that
Avraham kept all the mitzvos. The obvious question arises: wasn't
Yitzchak's own merit sufficient for him to deserve these blessings?

We find a similar statement later in the *parshah*.

וירא אליו ד' בלילה ההוא ויאמר אנכי אלקי אברהם
אביך אל תירא כי אתך אנכי וברכתיך והרביתי את
זרעך בעבור אברהם עבדי.

*God appeared to him that night and said, "I am the God of
your father, Avraham. Do not fear, for I am with you, and I
will bless you, and increase your seed, because of My servant, Avraham."*

(Bereishis 26:24)

Once again God assures Yitzchak that his seed will multiply because of the merit of his father, Avraham.

A great difference exists between one who creates something and one who follows that which already exists. Bringing into existence a concept that did not exist before is a
much greater achievement. Avraham, as the first one who
kept the mitzvos in their totality, brought into existence the
concept of mitzvah observance. We all are capable of keeping mitzvos because of our ability to emulate those who are
greater than we. Avraham was the initiator; all those who
followed only emulated. Thus, the Torah attributes the gift
of Eretz Yisrael and the increasing of the seed of Am Yisrael
to Avraham, whose achievement was on a different plane.

*   *   *

וישב יצחק ויחפר את בארת המים אשר חפרו בימי
אברהם אביו ויסתמום פלשתים אחרי מות אברהם
ויקרא להן שמות כשמת אשר קרא להן אביו.

*Yitzchak returned and dug the wells of water that had been
dug in the days of his father, Avraham, for the Plishtim had
stopped them up after Avraham's death. He gave them the
same names that his father had given them.*

(Bereishis 26:18)

Why did Yitzchak dig the same wells that his father Avraham dug, and why did he bestow the same names upon them?

Jews don't believe that the physical is intrinsically evil. Conversely, if used properly the world of the physical can raise one's spiritual level. Even more, when the physical is used in the proper fashion, not only does one's level of spirituality rise, but the physical objects themselves become holy.

Yitzchak understood that when Avraham used these wells, he used them with every aspect of purity, and therefore the wells themselves were holy. Thus, he wanted to rediscover the same wells that Avraham had used.

A name can indicate and symbolize the aspect of holiness existing in an object. The naming of the well *Be'er Shevah* in the time of Avimelech indicated and symbolized the treaty made between Avraham and Avimelech. Yitzchak used the same names used by Avraham, his father, because they indicated the aspects of the wells' holiness.

This, perhaps, is the source for why Chassidim eat their Rebbe's leftovers. They believe that since the Rebbe ate the food with pure intentions, the food itself is holy.

וn צא

Vayetzei

Why did Yaakov marry two sisters, an act prohibited by halachah? Didn't the Patriarchs keep the Torah even before it was given on Mt. Sinai?

The Torah states:

> דבר אל כל עדת בני ישראל ואמרת אלהם קדשים
> תהיו כי קדוש אני ד' אלקיכם.

Speak to the entire assembly of Bnei Yisrael and tell them,
"You shall be holy because I, the Lord, your God, am holy."
(Vayikra 19:2)

> הוו פרושים מן העריות ומן העבירה שכל מקום שאתה
> מוצא גדר ערוה אתה מוצא קדושה: אשה זונה וגו'
> אני ד' מקדשכם. ולא יחלל זרעו. אני ד' מקדשו
> קדושים יהיו. אשה זונה וחללה וגו'.
> (רש"י ד"ה קדושים תהיו)

Separate yourselves from prohibited relationships and from sin. For every time one finds a fence against licentiousness one find holiness, [as in the following examples]: "A woman that is a harlot or profaned," etc.; "I, the Lord, who sanctify you"; "And he shall not profane his seed...I am the Lord who sanctifies him";

"They shall be holy...a woman that is a harlot or pro-faned," etc.

(Rashi ad loc.)

Holiness, says Rashi, exists in opposition to the sins of licentiousness. To what holiness does Rashi refer?

One way to understand Rashi is to maintain that he is referring to the holiness of Eretz Yisrael, a holiness which prohibits licentiousness and indeed all the sins listed in the Torah. When Rashi says "from sin," he assumes that all sin depends on Eretz Yisrael's holiness. (This, in fact, is the position of the Ibn Ezra.) We can now understand the Ramban's explanation of why Yaakov could marry two sisters. The Patriarchs kept the Torah only in Eretz Yisrael, for only there could Torah find its ultimate fulfillment. Yaakov, outside of Eretz Yisrael, could therefore marry two sisters.

If fulfillment of mitzvos is contingent upon the holiness of Eretz Yisrael, why do we observe the mitzvos today outside of Israel?

ושמתם את דברי אלה על לבבכם ועל נפשכם...

You will place these, my words, within your hearts and within your souls...

(Devarim 11:18)

(ספרי) אף לאחר שתגלו היו מצויינים במצות הניחו
תפילין עשו מזוזות כדי שלא יהיו לכם חדשים כשתחזרו
וכן הוא אומר [ירמיה לא] הציבי לך ציונים.
(רש"י ד"ה ושמתם)

(Sifri) Even after you are exiled be careful with the mitzvos; put on tefillin, place mezuzos, so that they will not be new to you when you return, as it says "set up signposts for yourself" [Yirmiyahu 31:20].

(Rashi, ad loc.)

As we mentioned earlier, in *Parshas Bereishis*, Rashi explains that the reason for keeping the Torah outside of Eretz Yisrael is so that we will be used to their performance when we return. This explains the meaning of several other of Rashi's comments:

אני ד' אלוקיכם אשר הוצאתי אתכם מארץ מצרים
לתת לכם את ארץ כנען להיות לכם לאלקים.

I am the Lord, your God, who took you out of the land of Egypt to give you the land of Canaan, to be your God.

(Vayikra 25:38)

שכל הדר בארץ ישראל אני לו לאלקים וכל היוצא
ממנה כעובד ע"א.
(רש"י ד"ה להיות לכם)

That for he who lives in Eretz Yisrael, I am his God; and he who leaves it is like an idol-worshiper.

(Rashi, ad loc.)

ונתתי לך ולזרעך אחריך את ארץ מגריך את כל
ארץ כנען לאחזת עולם והייתי להם לאלקים.

And I will give to you and your offspring after you the land in which you dwell, all of the land of Canaan, as an eternal inheritance, and I will be your God.

(Bereishis 17:8)

ושם אהיה לכם לאלקים אבל הדר בחוצה לארץ כמו
שאין לו אלוק.
(רש"י ד"ה לאחוזת עולם)

And there I will be your God; but one who dwells outside of the land is like one who has no God.

(Rashi, ad loc.)

Rashi clearly says that only he who lives in Eretz Yisrael has a God. What is Rashi's meaning? We relate to God through the observance of His mitzvos. If their ultimate fulfillment can be only in Eretz Yisrael, the ultimate closeness to God can similarly be only in Eretz Yisrael.

The holiness referred to by Rashi can be explained also
as the holiness of *Am Yisrael*. It is this holiness that prohibits
certain relationships. This holiness came into being at the
time of *matan Torah*, as it says: "You will be for me a kingdom
of priests, a holy nation" (Shemos 19:6). With this understanding, again we can clearly see why Yaakov could marry
two sisters although the Patriarchs kept all the mitzvos though
they were not commanded to do so.

The Patriarchs kept the mitzvos that were sensible for
their time. However, if the reason for the mitzvah did not
exist, they did not keep it. Since the reason for keeping the
laws of prohibited relationships is dependent on the holiness
of *Am Yisrael*, a holiness that did not exist before *matan
Torah*, there was no reason for the Patriarchs to keep those
laws (other than those commanded to the Noachides).

According to this interpretation, when Rashi speaks of
"the sin" he is only referring to sins of licentiousness. This is
how the *Sifsei Chachamim* understands Rashi:

...ומן העבירות דנקט רש"י ר"ל נמי עבירות של
עריות.

(שפתי חכמים ויקרא יט:ב אות ב)

...From the sins that Rashi mentions, he means to say,
from the sins of licentiousness.
                              (*Sifsei Chachamim*, Vayikra 19:2)

This is also apparent from Rashi, since, in describing
holiness, all the examples he refers to relate to sins of licentiousness.

✳   ✳   ✳

וידר יעקב נדר לאמר אם יהיה אלקים עמדי ושמרני
בדרך הזה אשר אנכי הולך ונתן לי לחם לאכל
ובגד ללבש. ושבתי בשלום אל בית אבי והיה ד'
לי לאלקים. והאבן הזאת אשר שמתי מצבה יהיה
בית אלקים וכל אשר תתן לי עשר אעשרנו לך.

Yaakov made a vow, and said: "If God will be with me, and will guard me on this way that I go, and will give me bread to eat and clothing to wear, and I shall return in peace to my father's house, then the Lord shall be my God. And this stone that I have placed as a monument shall be a house of God, and of all that You give to me I shall give a tithe to You."

(Bereishis 28:20-22)

Yaakov vows that if God watches over him, in return he will make the altar a house of the Lord and give one-tenth of what he receives to God.

This vow of Yaakov seems quite strange. Does Yaakov dare make deals with God?

Before the giving of the Torah, every individual was expected to observe those commandments dictated by logic.

The Gemara states:

אמר ר' חנינא גדול מצווה ועושה ממי שאינו
מצווה ועושה.

Rav Chanina said, "One who is commanded and performs is greater than one who performs voluntarily."

(*Kiddushin* 31a)

Yaakov's intentions now become clear. If Yaakov had voluntarily made the altar into a house of the Lord and given one-tenth of what he earned, this would simply have been a voluntary gesture. But after he made his "deal," even before *matan Torah*, his promise became an obligation, for by logic one must honor one's vows. Therefore, Yaakov put himself in the state of one who is "commanded and performs," and so is considered greater.

*　　　　*　　　　*

ויאהב יעקב את רחל ויאמר אעבדך שבע שנים
ברחל בתך הקטנה.

Yaakov loved Rachel, and said, "I will work for you for
seven years for Rachel, your youngest daughter."
(Bereishis 29:18)

Why must the Torah specify that Yaakov loved Rachel?

ויבא גם אל רחל ויאהב גם את רחל מלאה ויעבד
עמו עוד שבע שנים אחרות.

And he also came to Rachel, and he also loved Rachel more
than Leah. And he worked with him another seven years.
(Bereishis 29:30)

The expression that the Torah uses, Yaakov "also loved
Rachel *more than* Leah," is ambiguous. The word *also* implies
that he loved Leah more; however, the words *more than* state
that he loved Rachel more. How can one understand this?

וילך ראובן בימי קציר חטים וימצא דודאים בשדה
ויבא אתם אל לאה אמו ותאמר רחל אל לאה תני נא
לי מדודאי בנך. ותאמר לה המעט קחתך את אישי
ולקחת גם את דודאי בני ותאמר רחל לכן ישכב עמך
הלילה תחת דודאי בנך.

Reuven went in the days of the wheat harvest and found
mandrakes in the field. He brought them to his mother,
Leah. Rachel said to Leah, "Please give me of your son's
mandrakes." She [Leah] said to her, "Is it not enough that
you took my husband, shall you also take my son's man-
drakes?" Rachel said, "Therefore, he shall lie with you tonight
in exchange for your son's mandrakes."
(Bereishis 30:14-15)

What is the meaning of the episode? Would Rachel
actually exchange her husband's presence for Reuven's flowers?

Leah's purpose in life was to be the primary physical creator
of the twelve tribes. She possessed unique personal charac-

teristics which were to be handed down to them. Her extraordi-
nary *midos* may be seen from Rashi's comment on the words:

ותרא רחל כי לא ילדה ליעקב ותקנא רחל באחתה
ותאמר אל יעקב הבה לי בנים ואם אין מתה אנכי.

*Rachel saw that she had not borne children to Yaakov, and
Rachel envied her sister, and said to Yaakov, "Give me sons,
and if not, I am dead."*

(Bereishis 30:1)

קנאה במעשיה הטובים אמרה אלולי שצדקה ממני לא
זכתה לבנים.

(רש"י ד"ה ותקנא רחל באחתה)

She envied her good deeds. She said, "If she were not
more righteous than I, she would not have merited sons."

(Rashi, ad loc.)

Even Rachel understood that it was Leah's special character traits that made her deserving of her children.

Leah should have given birth to even more tribes:

ואחר ילדה בת ותקרא את שמה דינה.

And afterwards she bore a daughter, and called her Dinah.

(Bereishis 30:21)

פירשו רבותינו שדנה לאה דין בעצמה אם זה זכר
לא תהא רחל אחותי כאחת השפחות והתפללה עליו
ונהפך לנקבה.

(רש"י ד"ה דינה)

Our Rabbis explained that Leah cast a judgment to herself: "If it is a male, my sister Rachel will not be even as the
maidservants." She prayed and it was changed to a female.

(Rashi, ad loc.)

It was actually due to God's mercy that Rachel had
children at all, as we see in Rashi:

ויזכר אלקים את רחל וישמע אליה אלקים
ויפתח את רחמה.

God remembered Rachel, and God listened to her and
opened her womb.

(Bereishis 30:22)

זכר לה שמסרה סימניה לאחותה...
(רש"י ד"ה ויזכור אלקים את רחל)

He remembered that she gave the signs to her sister...

(Rashi, ad loc.)

Rashi clearly states that because Rachel had mercy on Leah,
and gave her the signs that she had been given by Yaakov to identify
herself, God in turn had mercy on her and gave her children.

If Leah was destined to bear the tribes, it was Rachel on the
other hand, who was to educate them. Only a woman who has
special sensitivity to children can be their educator. That
woman was Rachel. This is clearly seen in the following verse:

וישלח יעקב ויקרא לרחל וללאה השדה אל צאנו.

Yaakov sent and called Rachel and Leah to the field, to his
flock.

(Bereishis 31:4)

לרחל תחלה ואח"כ ללאה שהיא היתה עקרת
הבית שבשבילה נזדווג יעקב עם לבן ואף בניה
של לאה מודים בדבר שהרי בועז ובית דינו משבט
יהודה אומרים כרחל וכלאה אשר בנו שתיהם וגו'
הקדימו רחל ללאה.

(רש"י ד"ה ויקרא לרחל וללאה)

First to Rachel and then to Leah, for she [Rachel] was
the *akeres habayis* [homemaker], for it was for her sake
that Yaakov joined Lavan. Even Leah's sons admitted
to this, for Boaz and his court, of the tribe of Yehudah,
said, "as Rachel and as Leah"... they placed Rachel
before Leah.

(Rashi, ad loc.)

Rachel is referred to as "*akeres habayis*," the one in charge of the household. This obviously does not mean she was a maid—rather, she was responsible for the upbringing of the tribes.

It is the deep affection a child has for a mother that enables her to influence her child. When Reuven brought the flowers to his natural mother, Leah, as a sign of affection, Rachel demanded those flowers. The affection had to be shown to her, as the educator of the tribes. Leah responded: If you are taking away my purpose of bearing the tribes by taking my husband, you can't have the flowers as well. You can't also be the educator. In return Rachel granted that Leah was correct, and exchanged living with Yaakov for the flowers—for the right to be the educator of the tribes.

The Torah points out that Yaakov loved Rachel, for that was a sign to the tribes that they should show their affection to Rachel, so she could be in the position to be their educator. The verse does not make clear whom Yaakov loved more, because the verse is referring to their separate purposes. Yaakov loved Leah more in regard to her purpose as bearer of the tribes; conversely, he loved Rachel more as their educator.

ותרא רחל כי לא ילדה ליעקב ותקנא רחל באחתה
ותאמר אל יעקב הבה לי בנים ואם אין מתה אנכי.
ויחר אף יעקב ברחל ויאמר התחת אלקים אנכי
אשר מנע ממך פרי בטן.

Rachel saw that she had not borne children to Yaakov, and Rachel envied her sister and told Yaakov, "Give me children, and if not, I am dead." Yaakov grew angry with Rachel, and said, "Am I in the place of God, who has withheld the fruit of the womb from you?"
(Bereishis 30:1-2)

את אמרת שאעשה כאבא אני איני כאבא אבא לא
היו לו בנים אני יש לי בנים מנע ממך ולא ממני.
(רש"י ד"ה אשר מנע ממך)

"You say that I should do as [my] father. I am not like [my]
father: [my] father had no children, and I have children.
He withheld them from you, and not from me."

(Rashi, ad loc.)

Rashi explains that Yaakov refused to pray for Rachel
because he himself had children and this was strictly her
problem. Yaakov's response seems very strange. Even if he
had children, didn't he have mercy for his beloved wife?

וישמע אלקים את קול הנער ויקרא מלאך אלקים
אל הגר מן השמים ויאמר לה מה לך הגר אל תיראי כי
שמע אלקים אל קול הנער באשר הוא שם.

*God heard the boy's voice. An angel of God called to Hagar
from heaven and said to her: "What is the matter, Hagar? Do
not fear, for God has heard the voice of the boy where he is."*

(Bereishis 21:17)

מכאן שיפה תפלת החולה מתפלת אחרים עליו
והיא קודמת להתקבל.

(רש"י ד"ה את קול הנער)

From here [we learn that] the prayers of the sick are
more beautiful than the prayers of others for him, and
are received more quickly.

(Rashi, ad loc.)

When Hagar and Yishmael cried to God to save him
from death, it was only Yishmael's prayers which were answered. Only the one who is actually in need can pray with
the proper intentions and repentance needed for his prayers
to be effective. Yaakov realized that his prayers would not
help, for his need was not as great as Rachel's. She had to
pray, because only her prayers would be answered.

Vayishlach

Several questions can be raised on this *parshah*.

קטנתי מכל החסדים ומכל האמת אשר עשית את עבדך
כי במקלי עברתי את הירדן הזה ועתה הייתי לשני
מחנות.

*I am unworthy of all the mercies and of all the truths that
You have shown Your servant. For with my stick I crossed
this Jordan, and now I am two camps.*

(Bereishis 32:11)

נתמעטו זכיותי ע"י החסדים והאמת שעשית עמי
לכך אני ירא שמא משהבטחתני נתלכלכתי בחטא
ויגרום לי להמסר ביד עשו.

(רש"י ד"ה קטנתי מכל החסדים)

My merits have become diminished by the mercies and
the truths that You have done with me. Therefore, I am
afraid lest since the time of Your promise to me I have
become defiled with sin, and this will cause me to fall
into Esav's hands.

(Rashi, ad loc.)

Rashi explains that Yaakov worried that because of all
the kindness God had shown him, he had become a sinner

and would be given over into Esav's hands. Yet, why should receiving kindness be an indication that one is a sinner; would not one think just the opposite?

וירא כי לא יכל לו ויגע בכף ירכו ותקע כף ירך יעקב
בהאבקו עמו. ויאמר שלחני כי עלה השחר ויאמר לא
אשלחך כי אם ברכתני.

He saw he could not prevail, and he touched the hollow of his thigh. The hollow of his thigh was put out of joint as he wrestled with him. He said: "Let me go, for dawn is breaking." And he said: "I shall not let you go unless you bless me."

(Bereishis 32:26-27)

Why was Yaakov wounded by the angel and why did he feel it necessary to receive a blessing from him? Furthermore, what kind of blessing is changing Yaakov's name to Yisrael?

ויאמר עשו אציגה נא עמך מן העם אשר אתי
ויאמר למה זה אמצא חן בעיני אדני.

Esav said: "Please let me leave with you some of the people that are with me." He [Yaakov] said: "For what reason? Let me find favor in the eyes of my lord."

(Bereishis 33:15)

Why did Yaakov refuse to take the servants that Esav offered him?

ויאמר לו אלקים שמך יעקב לא יקרא שמך עוד יעקב
כי אם ישראל יהיה שמך ויקרא את שמו ישראל.

God said to him: "Your name is Yaakov. Your name shall no longer be Yaakov; rather, Yisrael shall be your name." And He called him Yisrael.

(Bereishis 35:10)

Why was it necessary for God to repeat the angel's blessing to change Yaakov's name to Yisrael?

ויצו אתם לאמר כה תאמרון לאדני לעשו כה אמר
עבדך יעקב עם לבן גרתי ואחר עד עתה.

He commanded them, saying: "Thus shall you say to my
master, to Esav: 'Thus said your servant, Yaakov, "I have
sojourned with Lavan, and stayed there until now." ' "

(Bereishis 32:5)

...ד"א גרתי בגמטריא תרי"ג כלומר עם לבן הרשע
גרתי ותרי"ג מצות שמרתי ולא למדתי ממעשיו
הרעים.

(רש"י ד"ה גרתי)

...Another explanation: *garti* [I have sojourned] in *ge-*
matria is [equivalent to] *taryag* [613]; that is, I sojourned
with the wicked Lavan and kept the 613 mitzvos, and I
did not learn from his evil deeds.

(Rashi, ad loc.)

Finally, why does Yaakov insist on Esav being informed
that he had not been affected by Lavan and had kept all the
mitzvos. Why should the wicked Esav care?

The Gemara (*Kiddushin* 40b) states that God rewards the
wicked in this world so that they won't benefit in the World
to Come. Yaakov was worried: If he received so much good
from God, he must have done something wrong and therefore was receiving his reward in this world. For this reason he
had to be punished in this world and be physically hurt by
the angel.

For his blessing from the angel, Yaakov asked that the
benefits he would receive in this world not affect his *olam habah*.
The angel responds beautifully. If you remain Yaakov, the individual, then, like everyone else, the reward you receive in this
world will affect your *olam habah*. But if you are Yisrael—if you
are representing *Klal Yisrael*—nothing that happens in this world
will affect your World to Come, for it is God's deep desire to do
good to *Klal Yisrael* as a nation, in this world and the next.

For this same reason, Yaakov, as an individual, refuses to

benefit from Esav's gift of servants. And so he answers, "Let me find favor in the eyes of my lord" (Bereishis 33:15). Perhaps the words "my lord" refer to God, the true master. Yaakov wants to find favor in God's eyes, and so spurns benefits in this world.

After the sons of Yaakov took something for themselves personally, as it states: "The sons of Yaakov came onto the corpses, and plundered the city that had defiled their sister" (Bereishis 34:27), Yaakov must get still another blessing from God, that his World to Come should not be affected by this worldly benefit.

It now becomes clear why Yaakov wanted Esav to know that he had kept all the mitzvos. Only then could it be clear that the greatness he received in this world was not a result of his sin. He was not a sinner who had lost the right to form *Klal Yisrael*. Through these words Esav would realize that he could not destroy Yaakov.

וישב

Vayeshev

ותסר בגדי אלמנותה מעליה ותכס בצעיף ותתעלף
ותשב בפתח עינים אשר על דרך תמנתה כי ראתה כי
גדל שלה והוא לא נתנה לו לאשה.

*She [Tamar] took off her widow's garments, and covered
herself with a veil. She concealed herself, and sat at the entrance to Eynayim that was on the road to Timnah, for she saw
that Shelah had grown and she was not given to him as a wife.*
(Bereishis 38:14)

לפיכך הפקירה עצמה אצל יהודה שהיתה מתאוה
להעמיד ממנו בנים.

(רש"י ד"ה כי ראתה כי גדל שלה וגו')

She [Tamar] made herself free with Yehudah, for she
desired to bear children from him.

(Rashi, ad loc.)

Wasn't it prohibited for Tamar to live with her father-in-
law, Yehudah? And if we reply that Tamar was not obligated
to keep the mitzvos before *matan Torah*, we can still ask why
Yehudah, upon discovering that he had relations with Tamar,
declared that she was in the right, as it says:

ויכר יהודה ויאמר צדקה ממני כי על כן לא נתתיה
לשלה בני ולא יסף עוד לדעתה.

Yehudah recognized [her] and said, "She has been more
righteous than I; [she did this] because I did not give her to
my son, Shelah." And he was not intimate with her again.
(Bereishis 38:26)

There are two aspects to every mitzvah: the act itself and the
effect of the action. For example, within the obligation of *ma'aser*
one has the actual act of separation, and its effect—changing that
which was untithed and therefore forbidden into permitted produce. Similarly, the mitzvah of *yibum* comprises the act of having
relations and its consequent accomplishment—the birth of a
child who will be a remembrance for the deceased brother.

Before *matan Torah*, the acts of the mitzvos had no significance,
since they had not yet been demanded of the Jewish people. However, their effects still had significance and meaning. Before the
giving of the Torah, one who brought about desired consequences
was considered a *tzaddik*; one who did not was a *rasha*.

Sin also has two aspects—the act and the effect which
the Torah wishes to avoid. For example, in taking interest
there is the act of taking someone's money away and the
consequence, his loss. Before the giving of the Torah the act
itself was not prohibited, just the consequence of that act.

The greatness of the Patriarchs was that they performed the
acts that the Torah commands even before the giving of the
Torah. However, if the act and its effect contradicted each other,
before *matan Torah* the effect had more meaning, for it had
significance in and of itself, while the act itself was a *chumrah*
(stringency). Therefore, when the question arose as to which was
more important—not violating the prohibition of having relations
with one's father-in-law, or the accomplishment of bearing a child
who would establish a remembrance for the deceased husband, the
accomplishment took precedence. Thus, Tamar behaved correctly,
and Yehudah recognized the righteousness of her actions.

Miketz

וירא יוסף את אחיו ויכרם ויתנכר אלהם וידבר אתם
קשות ויאמר אלהם מאין באתם ויאמרו מארץ כנען
לשבר אכל. ויכר יוסף את אחיו והם לא הכרהו. ויזכר
יוסף את החלמות אשר חלם להם ויאמר אלהם
מרגלים אתם לראות את ערות הארץ באתם.

*Yosef saw his brothers and recognized them, but he made
himself strange to them and spoke harshly to them, and said:
"From where have you come?" They said: "From Eretz
Canaan, to buy food." Yosef recognized his brothers, but
they did not recognize him. Yosef remembered the dreams he
had dreamed about them, and he said: "You are spies who
have come to see the nakedness of the land."*

(Bereishis 42:7-9)

Weren't Yosef's harsh words to his brothers vengeful,
and thus prohibited? Furthermore, why, in the midst of the
discussion between Yosef and his brothers, does the *posuk*
interject that Yosef remembered his dreams?

שלחו מכם אחד ויקח את אחיכם ואתם האסרו
ויבחנו דבריכם האמת אתכם ואם לא חי פרעה
כי מרגלים אתם.

*Send one from among you, and he shall fetch your brother
and you shall be imprisoned, and your words shall be tested,
if there is truth in you; and if not, as Pharaoh lives, you are
spies.*

(Bereishis 42:16)

אם כנים אתם אחיכם אחד יאסר בבית משמרכם
ואתם לכו הביאו שבר רעבון בתיכם.

*If you are true men, let one of your brothers be imprisoned
in the house of your confinement, and you go, carry food to
your houses of famine.*

(Bereishis 42:19)

If Yosef was testing the truth of his brothers intentions to
see if they were spying or merely coming to buy food, why did
he give them food even before they came back with Binyamin?

When Yosef's dreams came true, he realized he was to be
the next link in the creation of *Am Yisrael.* Therefore, he had
to teach his brothers to subjugate themselves to him so that
he would be recognized as the source from which everyone
should learn. Before Yosef's harsh words to his brothers, the
Torah explains why he spoke so—he realized he was the one
everybody must subjugate themselves to, so that he would be
able to educate them. This also explains why he gave them
food even before they brought back Binyamin. Again, this
caused his brothers to feel obligated and subjugated to him.

This explains still another question as well.

ואת גביעי גביע הכסף תשים בפי אמתחת הקטן
ואת כסף שברו ויעש כדבר יוסף אשר דבר.

*"And my cup, the silver cup, place in the pack of the
youngest, and his money for food." And he did according to
the words that Yosef had spoken.*

(Bereishis 44:2)

Didn't Yosef have the power to take Binyamin prisoner without going through the entire plot of planting a cup in his sack and accusing him of stealing it? Yosef realized that his brothers would never subjugate themselves to him if they felt God was with them, if they still had *siyata dishmaya* (the help of Heaven). Therefore, Yosef created a situation to show the brothers that God was with him and not with them. This is beautifully expressed by Rashi later, when Binyamin is caught with the cup:

ויאמר יהודה מה נאמר לאדני מה נדבר ומה נצטדק
האלקים מצא את עון עבדיך הננו עבדים לאדני גם
אנחנו גם אשר נמצא הגביע בידו.

Yehudah said: "What shall we say to my lord? What shall we speak? And how shall we justify ourselves? The Lord has discovered your servants' sin. Behold, we are my lord's slaves, we as well as the one with whom the cup is found."
(Bereishis 44:16)

יודעים אנו שלא סרחנו אבל מאת המקום נהיתה
להביא לנו זאת מצא בעל חוב מקום לגבות שטר חובו.
(רש"י ד"ה האלקים מצא)

We know that we have done no wrong, but it is from the Lord that this came upon us. The creditor has found a place to collect his debt.

(Rashi, ad loc.)

*   *   *

שלחו מכם אחד ויקח את אחיכם ואתם האסרו ויבחנו
דבריכם האמת אתכם ואם לא חי פרעה כי מרגלים
אתם. ויאסף אתם אל משמר שלשת ימים. ויאמר
אלהם יוסף ביום השלישי זאת עשו וחיו את האלקים
אני ירא. אם כנים אתם אחיכם אחד יאסר בבית
משמרכם ואתם לכו הביאו שבר רעבון בתיכם.

"Send one from among you, and he shall fetch your brother and you shall be imprisoned, and your words shall be tested,

if there is truth in you; and if not, as Pharaoh lives, you are spies." He put them into custody for three days. Yosef told them on the third day: "This you shall do, and live; I fear God. If you are true men, let one of your brothers be imprisoned in the house of your confinement, and you go, carry food to your houses of famine."

(Bereishis 42:16-19)

Why did Yosef change from demanding that only one brother go fetch Binyamin to saying that all the brothers besides Shimon could go?

The tribes were not willing to leave only one brother by himself with Yosef. Therefore, at first only one was going to fetch Binyamin. But as soon as Yosef declared that he feared God, they realized that they could trust Yosef with Shimon alone.

ויגש

Vayigash

ויאמר אלקים לישראל במראת הלילה ויאמר יעקב
יעקב ויאמר הנני.

God spoke to Yisrael in the visions of the night, and said:
"Yaakov, Yaakov," and he said, "Here I am."

(Bereishis 46:2)

Why does the verse begin with Yisrael and end with Yaakov?

אנכי ארד עמך מצרימה ואנכי אעלך גם עלה
ויוסף ישית ידו על עיניך.

I will go down with you to Egypt, and I will bring you up
again. And Yosef will place his hand upon your eyes.

(Bereishis 46:4)

הבטיחו להיות נקבר בארץ.

(רש"י ד"ה ואנכי אעלך)

He promised he would be buried in Eretz [Yisrael].

(Rashi, ad loc.)

Why was it so important to Yaakov to be buried in Eretz
Yisrael?

וַיֹּאמֶר יִשְׂרָאֵל אֶל יוֹסֵף אָמוּתָה הַפָּעַם אַחֲרֵי רְאוֹתִי
אֶת פָּנֶיךָ כִּי עוֹדְךָ חָי.

*Yisrael said to Yosef: "Now I can die, after I have seen your
face, for you are still alive."*

(Bereishis 46:30)

וַיֵּשֶׁב יִשְׂרָאֵל בְּאֶרֶץ מִצְרַיִם בְּאֶרֶץ גֹּשֶׁן וַיֵּאָחֲזוּ בָהּ וַיִּפְרוּ
וַיִּרְבּוּ מְאֹד.

*Yisrael lived in the land of Egypt, in the land of Goshen.
They took possession of it, and were fruitful.*

(Bereishis 47:27)

Why is Yaakov referred to as Yisrael in these two verses?

As I mentioned in *Parshas Vayishlach*, whenever the Torah
uses the name Yaakov, it refers to Yaakov as an individual.
When the Torah calls him Yisrael, it is in his role as representative of *Klal Yisrael*.

Ma'aras Hamachpelah (the Cave of Machpelah, burial
ground of the Patriarchs) symbolizes the foundations of *Klal
Yisrael*: Adam and Chavah, the physical foundations, and the
Patriarchs, the foundations of *Klal Yisrael*'s spiritual characteristics. Yaakov feared that he had lost his *olam haba*, and
his chance to be one of the foundations of *Klal Yisrael*:

...סָבוּר הָיִיתִי לָמוּת שְׁתֵּי מִיתוֹת בָּעוֹה"ז וְלָעוֹה"ב
שֶׁנִּסְתַּלְּקָה מִמֶּנִּי שְׁכִינָה וְהָיִיתִי אוֹמֵר שֶׁיִּתְבָּעֵנִי הַקָּבָּ"ה
מִיתָתְךָ עַכְשָׁיו שֶׁעוֹדְךָ חָי לֹא אָמוּת אֶלָּא פַּעַם אַחַת.
(רש"י בראשית מו:ל ד"ה אמותה הפעם)

...I had been certain I would die two deaths, in this
world and in the World to Come, for the Presence had
left me. I had said that the Holy One, blessed be He,
would hold me responsible for your death. Now that
you are still alive I shall only die once.

(Rashi, Bereishis 46:30)

Because Yaakov believed that he had lost his *olam haba*
and his chance to be a foundation of *Klal Yisrael*, due to the

death of Yosef, it was important for him to be guaranteed that he would be buried in *Ma'aras Hamachpelah*—a clear indication that he was, indeed, a founder of *Klal Yisrael*.

This also explains why God referred to him as both Ya-akov and Yisrael. God called him by the name of Yaakov, for that was how Yaakov saw himself—as an individual. But in truth he was the foundation of *Klal Yisrael*, for Yosef was not dead—and thus he was called Yisrael as well. When Yaakov met Yosef and realized that he was alive, the Torah calls him Yisrael, for now he understood that he would be the foundation of *Klal Yisrael*. And, finally, when the *parshah* comes to an end with the idea of the growth of *Klal Yisrael* in Egypt, it naturally refers to him as Yisrael, for here we see *Klal Yisrael* coming into existence.

ויחי

Vayechi

ויחי יעקב בארץ מצרים שבע עשרה שנה ויהי ימי
יעקב שני חייו שבע שנים וארבעים ומאת שנה. ויקרבו
ימי ישראל למות ויקרא לבנו ליוסף ויאמר לו אם נא
מצאתי חן בעיניך שים נא ידך תחת ירכי ועשית עמדי
חסד ואמת אל נא תקברני במצרים.

*Yaakov lived in the land of Egypt seventeen years, and the
days of Yaakov, the years of his life, were one hundred and
forty-seven years. The day of Yisrael's death approached,
and he called to his son, to Yosef, and said to him, "If I have
found favor in your eyes, please put your hand beneath my
thigh, and show me a kindness and truth; do not bury me in
Egypt."*

(Bereishis 47:28-29)

Why does the Torah here, and in many other verses
throughout the *parshah*, start off using the name Yaakov and
then switch to Yisrael?

ושכבתי עם אבתי ונשאתני ממצרים וקברתני
בקברתם ויאמר אנכי אעשה כדברך. ויאמר
השבעה לי וישבע לו וישתחו ישראל על ראש
המטה.

*"I shall lie with my ancestors, and you shall carry me from
Egypt, and bury me in their burial place." And he [Yosef]
said, "I shall do according to your words." He [Yaakov]
said, "Swear to me," and he swore to him. And Yisrael
bowed at the head of the bed.*

(Bereishis 47:30-31)

When Yaakov requested that Yosef bury him in Eretz
Yisrael, Yosef immediately answered that he would fulfill his
father's request. But although Yosef responds positively, Yaakov demands that he swear. Why did Yaakov demand a
second commitment through a vow? Didn't he trust his son?

ויגד ליעקב ויאמר הנה בנך יוסף בא אליך ויתחזק
ישראל וישב על המטה.

*One told Yaakov, and said: "Behold, your son Yosef has come
to you." Yisrael strengthened himself and sat on the bed.*
(Bereishis 48:2)

Again, why does the verse begin with the name Yaakov
and then switch to Yisrael?

וירא ישראל את בני יוסף ויאמר מי אלה.

Yisrael saw Yosef's sons and said, "Who are these?"
(Bereishis 48:8)

מהיכן יצאו אלו שאינן ראוין לברכה.
(רש"י ד"ה ויאמר מי אלה)

From where do these come, who are not worthy of a
blessing?

(Rashi, ad loc.)

Rashi explains that Yaakov questioned the worthiness of
Efrayim and Menashe to receive the blessings. Why would Yaakov raise this point after he had already given a blessing to
them, as it says:

ועתה שני בניך הנולדים לך בארץ מצרים עד באי
אליך מצרימה לי הם אפרים ומנשה כראובן ושמעון
יהיו לי.

*Now, the two sons born to you in the land of Egypt until I
came to you to Egypt, they are mine, Efrayim and Menashe
shall be to me as Reuven and Shimon.*

(Bereishis 48:5)

Finally, we find still another verse that uses the names of
Yaakov and Yisrael:

הקבצו ושמעו בני יעקב ושמעו אל ישראל אביכם.

*Gather together and listen, sons of Yaakov, and listen to
your father, Yisrael.*

(Bereishis 49:2)

If one understands that when the Torah uses the term
Yaakov it refers to Yaakov the individual, and when it uses
the term Yisrael, it refers to the representative of *Klal Yisrael*,
all these questions can be resolved. The *parshah* starts off
with Yaakov, the individual, dying, and that period of the
formation of *Klal Yisrael* coming to an end. That's why the
double expression of Yaakov and Yisrael. When Yosef answers that he will bury him—Yaakov—in Eretz Yisrael, Yaakov immediately responds: I don't want you to agree to bury
me there as a son listening to his father; I want you to
understand that my being buried in Ma'aras Hamachpelah has
meaning for *Klal Yisrael*, and you must do it as an obligation
to them. With my passing away there is the culmination of
the *midos* of the Patriarchs, who are symbolized by Ma'aras
Hamachpelah. And so the Torah refers to him as Yisrael
when discussing this vow: "He swore to him. And Yisrael
bowed at the head of the bed" (Bereishis 47:31).

Later, when Yosef visits Yaakov, the Torah begins with
the name Yaakov. Yaakov as an individual, as a father to a
son, had no obligation to sit up for Yosef. But Yaakov as

representative of a part of *Klal Yisrael* that is coming to an end must sit up for *Klal Yisrael*'s new representative. Therefore the verse changes to the name Yisrael.

When Yaakov said that Efrayim and Menashe "shall be to me as Reuven and Shimon" (Bereishis 48:5), his blessing was that of a grandfather to his grandchildren. A grandfather may give a blessing even if his grandchildren are not worthy. But later, when it comes to giving the blessing of *Klal Yisrael*, the blessing of: "In you shall Yisrael bless, and say, 'May God make you as Efrayim and as Menashe'" (Bereishis 48:20)—the blessing which represents what every Jew should be—it is concerning this blessing that Yisrael, representative of the nation, asks: "Who are they? Are they worthy of such a blessing?"

This also explains the verse: "Gather together and listen, sons of Yaakov, and listen to your father, Yisrael" (Bereishis 49:2). There were two sets of blessings. First, there were the blessings of a father to his sons. A father may not withhold his blessing from some sons and not others, or even differentiate between sons. Second, there were the blessings of the formation of *Klal Yisrael*—the blessings of Yisrael. At this time each got the blessing appropriate for him. This is clear from Rashi at the end of the *parshah*:

כל אלה שבטי ישראל שנים עשר וזאת אשר דבר
להם אביהם ויברך אותם איש אשר כברכתו ברך
אתם.

All these are the twelve tribes of Yisrael, and this is what their father said to them, and he blessed them, each man according to his blessing he blessed them.

(Bereishis 49:28)

והלא יש מהם שלא ברכם אלא קנטרן אלא כך פירושו
וזאת אשר דבר להם אביהם מה שנאמר בענין יכול
שלא ברך לראובן שמעון ולוי ת"ל ויברך אותם כולם
במשמע.

(רש"י ד"ה וזאת אשר דבר להם)

And were not among them those he did not bless, but
rather reproached? However, this is what it means: [The
words] "this is what their father said to them" [imply]
all that was said in the matter [i.e., the reproach]. [But
you may think that] he did not bless Reuven, Shimon,
and Levi [at all]. Therefore the Scripture says "he blessed
them"—implying all of them.

(Rashi, ad loc.)

Rashi declares that Reuven, Shimon, and Levi received
blessings, yet we see that Yaakov, in fact, rebuked them.
What Rashi means is that there were two sets of blessings:
the blessings of Yaakov, father to his sons, in which everyone
was blessed, and the blessings of Yisrael, in which everyone
received the blessing they deserved.

*   *   *

וימלאו לו ארבעים יום כי כן ימלאו ימי החנטים ויבכו
אתו מצרים שבעים יום.

*Forty days were fulfilled for him, for so is fulfilled the days of
the embalming, and the Egyptians wept for him seventy
days.*

(Bereishis 50:3)

ארבעים לחניטה ושלשים לבכיה...
(רש"י ד"ה ויבכו אותו וגו')

Forty days for embalming, and thirty for weeping...

(Rashi, ad loc.)

ויבאו עד גרן האטד אשר בעבר הירדן ויספדו שם
מספד גדול וכבד מאד ויעש לאביו אבל שבעת ימים.

*They came to the threshing floor of Atad that was on the
other side of the Jordan, and they made a very great and
bitter eulogy, and he made a mourning for his father for
seven days.*

(Bereishis 50:10)

Why was it necessary for Yisrael's children to leave Egypt to mourn their father? Couldn't they have mourned together with the Egyptians in Egypt?

There is a clear distinction between the mourning of a Jew and that of a non-Jew. The mourning of a non-Jew is a destructive act: he merely cries and sinks into depression. Conversely, the mourning of a Jew is a constructive act: he realizes that everything is vanity and uses this insight to better himself. For this very reason we find that cutting oneself over a dead person as the non-Jews used to do is forbidden as a destructive act. Yisrael's children would not observe their mourning in Egypt, for there the mourning was destructive, while they wanted to observe a constructive mourning.

Similarly, in the mourning of Egypt the Torah states that they cried, a destructive act, but in the mourning of Yosef and his brothers the verse says they eulogized. The purpose of a eulogy is to talk about the deceased and awaken those who are listening to repentance, a constructive act.

Yosef and his brothers mourned seven days while the Egyptians mourned for thirty, because since the mourning of a Jew is a constructive act, the main part of it is limited to seven days. Now one has to act upon what he has learned—and not just continue weeping.

*   *   *

ויברכם ביום ההוא לאמור בך יברך ישראל לאמר ישמך אלקים כאפרים וכמנשה וישם את אפרים לפני מנשה.

He blessed them on that day, and said, "In you shall Yisrael bless, to say: 'May God make you as Efrayim and as Menashe,'" and he placed Efrayim before Menashe.
(Bereishis 48:20)

הבא לברך את בניו יברכם בברכתם ויאמר איש לבנו
ישימך אלקים כאפרים וכמנשה.
(רש"י ד"ה בך יברך ישראל)

Whoever goes to bless his children will give them their
blessing, and a man shall say to his son, "May God make
you as Efrayim and as Menashe."

(Rashi, ad loc.)

Yaakov blessed Efrayim and Menashe with the ultimate blessing: that *Klal Yisrael* would bestow its blessing with the hope that
their sons would be like Efrayim and Menashe. But why doesn't
the Torah describe their greatness, as it does with the other tribes?
Furthermore, how does Rashi know the Torah is referring to the
blessing of a parent to his son? Perhaps it is referring to blessings
between friends or a teacher and his students?

History has shown that each generation is not as great as
the previous one, for it is very difficult for one generation to
absorb everything it has been exposed to by its predecessors.
How beautifully, then, does Yaakov describe the greatness of
Efrayim and Menashe:

...אפרים ומנשה כראובן ושמעון יהיו לי.

...Efrayim and Menashe shall be to me as Reuven and Shimon.
(Bereishis 48:5)

Efrayim and Menashe were the exceptions, the ones who
attained everything that the previous generation had to offer.

Now it becomes clear why Rashi declares that the blessing "In you shall Yisrael bless" applies to a parent blessing his
child. This is the older generation blessing the younger, that
they, like Efrayim and Menashe, should incorporate into
their personalities everything they have been exposed to.

YAMIM TOVIM

Rosh Hashanah
and Yom Kippur

The Concept of Teshuvah

The concept of *teshuvah*, repentance, seems to be an illogical one. True, a sinner must change his ways: One who wishes to avoid incurring further punishment must clearly cease his sinning. Yet by what logic can a previous sin be forgiven? If one changes for the better, should he not still receive the punishment he deserves for the bad that he has done, as well as the reward he deserves for the good he is currently doing?

One might answer that since Hashem is all-merciful, in His mercy He wipes away our sins even though logically He has no reason to do so.

כל מי שניחם על המצות שעשה ותהה על הזכיות ואמר
בלבו ומה הועלתי בעשייתן הלואי לא עשיתי אותן הרי
זה איבד את כולן ואין מזכירים לו שום זכות בעולם
שנאמר וצדקת הצדיק לא תצילנו ביום רשעו אין זה
אלא בתוהה על הראשונות...

> Whoever regrets the mitzvos he has fulfilled and wonders
> at his meritorious deeds, and says to himself: "What did I
> get out of doing them? Would that I had not done
> them," loses all of them, and no merit is remembered in
> his favor, as it says: The righteousness of the righteous
> shall not save him on the day of his wickedness—this is if
> he regrets his original [good deeds]...
>
> (Rambam, *Hilchos Teshuvah* 3:3)

This insight of the Rambam proves that Hashem's "forgetting" our past is not merely a question of His mercy, for the concept can work against a man as well—one who regrets his past righteousness loses his accumulated reward. Surely, this is not an example of God's mercy.

When God judges an individual, He does not simply weigh his sins and mitzvos on a scale, with a *rasha* being one whose sins are "heavier." Rather, Hashem makes His judgment on the individual himself. What is he? What does he represent? Is he the embodiment of good or of evil? True, a person's essential being will depend upon the mitzvos and sins that he has done, but he is actually judged for the gestalt of his being, the whole and not the parts.

When a person truly regrets his past actions, he is stating that this period in his life does not embody him. When being judged for what he represents, those sins or those mitzvos that he regrets are not factors in judgment, since they do not represent him anymore.

This understanding of how God judges an individual is apparent in the Rambam:

בשעה ששוקלין עונות אדם עם זכיותיו אין מחשבין
עליו עון שחטא בו תחלה ולא שני אלא משלישי
ואילך אם נמצאו עונותיו משלישי ואילך מרובין על
זכיותיו אותם שתי עונות מצטרפים ודנין אותו על
הכל. ואם נמצאו זכיותיו כנגד עונותיו אשר מעון
שלישי ואילך מעבירים כל עונותיו ראשון ראשון. לפי
שהשלישי נחשב ראשון שכבר נמחלו השנים. וכן
הרביעי הרי הוא ראשון שכבר נמחל השלישי וכן
עד סופן...

When a person's sins and merits are weighed, the first
sin that he sinned is not counted, nor the second, but
the third and on [are counted]. If it is found that his
sins—from the third and on—are greater than his merits, the [first] two sins are included and he is judged on
them all. But if his merits stand against his sins, each of
his sins is cancelled one by one. The third is considered
as the first, for the first two were forgiven. And thus the
fourth becomes the first, for after all the third has been
forgiven, and so on to the end...

(Rambam, *Hilchos Teshuvah* 3:5)

According to the Rambam, when calculating our sins
against our mitzvos, Hashem does not count the first two
times we sin. Bearing our explanation of *teshuvah* in mind,
the reason for this is quite clear. The Gemara considers that
an action must occur three times to establish a status quo (a
chazakah). The first two times a person sins he had not
indicated that he is a person who embodies that particular
transgression. He simply is one who gave in to his evil inclination. Only after he transgresses three times can one say
that he represents the sin itself, and as such can be judged for
his embodiment of the evil, not for one particular sin.

מדרכי התשובה להיות השב צועק תמיד לפני השם
בבכי ובתחנונים ועושה צדקה כפי כחו ומתרחק הרבה
מן הדבר שחטא בו ומשנה שמו כלומר אני אחר ואיני
אותו האיש שעשה אותן המעשים ומשנה מעשיו כולן
לטובה ולדרך ישרה וגולה ממקומו...

Some of the ways of repentance are for the penitent to
constantly shout before Hashem, with tears and pleas;
to give as much charity as is in his power; to distance
himself from the object of his sin; and to change his
name, as if to say: I am another, and am not the same
person who did those deeds. He changes his actions
entirely for the better, onto the straight path, and exiles
himself from his former place of residence...

(Rambam, *Hilchos Teshuvah* 2:4)

How can the Rambam write that one should change his name and say he is someone else? According to our explanation this is exactly the point of *teshuvah*. One must declare that the periods and moments of one's life spent in sin do not represent him. He is a different person, represented by mitzvos, not by sins.

שעיר המשתלח לפי שהוא כפרה על כל ישראל כהן
גדול מתודה עליו על לשון כל ישראל שנאמר והתודה
עליו את כל עונות בני ישראל. שעיר המשתלח מכפר
על כל עבירות שבתורה הקלות והחמורות. בין שעבר
בזדון בין שעבר בשגגה. בין שהודע לו בין שלא
הודע לו הכל מתכפר בשעיר המשתלח. והוא שעשה
תשובה. אבל אם לא עשה תשובה אין השעיר
מכפר לו אלא על הקלות. ומה הן הקלות ומה הן
החמורות. החמורות הן שחייבין עליהם מיתת
בית דין או כרת. ושבועת שוא ושקר אע"פ שאין
בהן כרת הרי הן מן החמורות. ושאר מצות לא
תעשה ומצות עשה שאין בהן כרת הם הקלות.

Because the scapegoat is an atonement for all of Yisrael, the High Priest made confession over it in the name of all of Yisrael, as it says: "He will confess over it all the transgressions of *Bnei Yisrael*." The scapegoat atones for all the sins in the Torah, the light sins and the more severe, those transgressed purposely, and those transgressed accidentally, those he was aware of and those he was not aware of—all is atoned through the scapegoat, provided one repented. But if he did not repent, the scapegoat does not atone for him, except for the light sins. What is the difference between the lighter and the more severe? The more severe are those that make transgressors liable for judicial sentence of death or *kareis* [excision]. Oaths taken in vain and lies, although they are not punishable by *kareis*, are among the more severe. The other negative and positive precepts that are not punishable by *kareis* are the lighter ones.

(Rambam, *Hilchos Teshuvah* 1:2)

How could the scapegoat atone for "light" sins without the sinner's repentance? This is especially difficult to understand in light of the Rambam's words in the previous halachah:

וכן בעלי חטאות ואשמות בעת שמביאין קרבנותיהן...
על שגגתן או על זדונן אין מתכפר להן בקרבנם עד
שיעשו תשובה. ויתודו וידוי דברים שנאמר והתודה
אשר חטא עליה. וכן כל מחוייבי מיתות בית דין
ומחוייבי מלקות אין מתכפר להן במיתתן או בלקייתן
עד שיעשו תשובה ויתודו. וכן החובל בחבירו והמזיק
ממונו אף על פי ששילם לו מה שהוא חייב לו אינו
מתכפר עד שיתודה וישוב מלעשות כזה לעולם שנאמר
מכל חטאות האדם.

...Those who bring sin-offerings and guilt-offerings, at the time that they bring their sacrifices for sins committed accidentally or willfully, are not forgiven through their sacrifices until they have repented. They must make oral confession, as it says: "He shall confess that which he sinned on it." Similarly, all who are liable for capital punishment or flogging are not atoned for by their deaths or lashing until they have repented and confessed. Similarly, one who wounds his fellow, or damages him monetarily, even if he has paid what is due, is not atoned for until he has confessed and penitently resolves not to do so again forever, as it says, "from all the sins of the men."

(Rambam, *Hilchos Teshuvah* 1:1)

The Mishnah says that since those exiled in the cities of sanctuary were released only upon the death of the High Priest, the High Priest's mother used to feed and clothe the exiles so they wouldn't pray for her son's death.

לפיכך אימותיהן של כהנים מספקות להן מחיה וכסות כדי
שלא יתפללו על בניהם שימותו...טעמא דלא מצלו הא מצלו
מייתי והכתיב כצפור לנוד כדרור לעוף כן קללת חנם לא
תבא [אמר ההוא] סבא מפירקיה דרבא שמיע לי שהיה להן
לבקש רחמים על דורן ולא בקשו.

Therefore the mothers of priests gave them food and clothing, so that they not pray that their sons die...The reason [the High Priest did not die] is because they [the exiles] didn't pray. If they would have prayed would they have died? Yet it says, "As a bird by wandering, as a bat by flying, so a curse shall not come without cause." Said a venerable old scholar: I heard an explanation at one of the lectures of Rabba, that they should have implored Divine grace for the generation, which they failed to do.

(*Makos* 11a)

The High Priest bears partial responsibility for whatever happens in his generation. Had he prayed properly, he could have prevented those accidental murders. A similar concept is found in Rashi:

למה נסמכה מיתת מרים לפרשת פרה אדומה לומר
לך מה קרבנות מכפרין אף מיתת צדיקים מכפרת.
(רש"י במדבר כ:א ד"ה ותמת שם מרים)

Why does the section on Miriam's death follow the section on the red heifer? To tell you that just as sacrifices atone, so the death of the righteous atones.

(Rashi, Bamidbar 20:1)

The death of a righteous man atones because he is being held responsible for the wrongdoings of his generation. If he had been a better example, perhaps fewer people would have sinned.

The High Priest's confession on behalf of *Klal Yisrael*, the Rambam points out, was an integral part of the service of the scapegoat. Every individual doesn't have to repent for the light sins that will be atoned for; the one held responsible for them, the High Priest, repents for his entire generation.

*   *   *

בזמן הזה שאין בית המקדש קיים ואין לנו מזבח כפרה
אין שם אלא תשובה. התשובה מכפרת על כל העבירות.
אפילו רשע כל ימיו ועשה תשובה באחרונה אין מזכירין לו
שום דבר מרשעו שנאמר רשעת הרשע לא יכשל בה ביום
שובו מרשעו. ועצמו של יום הכפורים מכפר לשבים
שנאמר כי ביום הזה יכפר עליכם.

Today, when the Beis Hamikdash no longer exists, and
we have no altar, nothing is left but repentance, and
repentance atones for all sins. Even if one was wicked
all his life, and in the end repented, his wickedness is
not recalled to him, as it says: "The wickedness of the
wicked will not cause him to stumble on the day he
repents from his evil." The day of Yom Kippur itself
atones for the penitent, as it says: "For on this day it
shall atone for you."

(Rambam, Hilchos Teshuvah 1:3)

אף על פי שהתשובה מכפרת על הכל ועצמו של יום
הכפורים מכפר. יש עבירות שהן מתכפרים לשעתן ויש
עבירות שאין מתכפרים אלא לאחר זמן. כיצד עבר אדם
על מצות עשה שאין בה כרת ועשה תשובה אינו זז משם
עד שמוחלין לו ובאלו נאמר שובו בנים שובבים ארפא
משובותיכם וגו'. עבר על מצות לא תעשה שאין בה
כרת ולא מיתת בית דין ועשה תשובה. תשובה תולה
ויום הכפורים מכפר ובאלו נאמר כי ביום הזה
יכפר עליכם. עבר על כריתות ומיתות בית דין
ועשה תשובה. תשובה ויום הכפורים תולין ויסורין
הבאין עליו גומרין לו הכפרה. ולעולם אין מתכפר
לו כפרה גמורה עד שיבואו עליו יסורין ובאלו
נאמר ופקדתי בשבט פשעם ובנגעים עונם. במה דברים
אמורים בשלא חילל את השם בשעה שעבר אבל המחלל
את השם אע"פ שעשה תשובה והגיע יום הכפורים
והוא עומד בתשובתו ובאו עליו יסורין אינו מתכפר
לו כפרה גמורה עד שימות. אלא תשובה יום הכפורים
ויסורין שלשתן תולין ומיתה מכפרת שנאמר ונגלה באזני
ד' צבקות וגו' אם יכופר העון הזה לכם עד תמותון.

Although repentance atones for everything and Yom
Kippur itself atones, there are some sins that are atoned
for immediately, and others that are atoned for only
after time has elapsed. For example: a man committed a

transgression of a positive commandment for which he
is not liable for the punishment of *kareis*, and repented—
he is forgiven immediately. Of these it is said: "Return,
wandering sons, I will heal you..." If he violated a negative commandment for which he is not liable *kareis* or
capital punishment, and he repented, his repentance
remains pending and Yom Kippur atones. Of these it is
said: "For on this day it shall atone for you." If he
committed transgressions for which he is liable *kareis* or
capital punishment, and repented, his repentance and
Yom Kippur remain pending and suffering comes upon
him to complete the atonement. He does not achieve
complete atonement until the suffering has come upon
him, and of these it is said: "I shall remember their sin
with a rod, and with affliction their iniquity." These
things refer to one who did not desecrate the Name at
the time he transgressed. But if one desecrated the
Name, although he repented, and Yom Kippur arrived
and he was firm in his repentance, and suffering came
upon him, he will not achieve complete atonement until
death. Repentance, Yom Kippur, and suffering—the three
remain pending and death atones, as it says: "It will be
revealed in the ears of the Lord of Hosts...if this sin will
be atoned until you have died."

(Rambam, Hilchos Teshuvah 1:4)

The Rambam states that the day of Yom Kippur itself
atones. He is clearly not referring to the suffering of the
day—the prohibition of eating, drinking, washing oneself,
etc.—since suffering is classified as a separate means of
atonement.

הלל ושמאי קבלו מהם. הלל אומר הוי מתלמידיו של אהרן
אוהב שלום ורודף שלום אוהב את הבריות ומקרבן לתורה

Hillel and Shammai received from them. Hillel used to
say: "Be among the students of Aharon, loving peace
and pursuing peace, loving people and bringing them
close to Torah."

(Avos 1:12)

R. Ovadiah of Bartenura asks: How did Aharon bring people closer to Torah? His response:

> כשהיה יודע באדם שעבר עבירה היה מתחבר עמו...ומראה
> לו פנים צהובות. והיה אותו אדם מתבייש ואומר אילו
> היה יודע צדיק זה מעשי הרעים כמה היה מתרחק ממני
> ומתוך כך היה חוזר למוטב, הוא שהנביא מעיד עליו
> (מלאכי ב') בשלום ובמישור הלך אתי ורבים השיב מעון.

When he knew that a person had sinned he would befriend him...That person would feel ashamed and say, "If this tzaddik knew my evil deeds, how he would distance himself from me," and from this he would return to acting properly. This is what the prophet attests to (Malachi 2:6), "He walked with me in peace and uprightness, and turned many away from iniquity."

(Bartenura ad loc.)

During the period between Rosh Hashanah and Yom Kippur God comes closer to us. This is clearly stated in the Rambam:

> אע"פ שהתשובה והצעקה יפה לעולם. בעשרה הימים שבין
> ראש השנה ויום הכפורים היא יפה ביותר ומתקבלת היא
> מיד שנאמר דרשו ד' בהמצאו [קראהו בהיותו קרוב]...

Although repentance and supplication are always good, they are particularly so in the ten days between Rosh Hashanah and Yom Kippur, and they are immediately accepted, as it says: "Search for the Lord where He is to be found, [call Him when He is close]..."

(Rambam, *Hilchos Teshuvah* 2:6)

God's closeness allows this period to be a more opportune time for *teshuvah*. When Hashem comes near to us we feel undeserving of this closeness. This causes us to examine our deeds and repent, as it did to those approached by Aharon.

However, the question still remains: How is the day itself an atonement, exclusive of our own repentance?

Rabbi Moshe Chaim Luzzatto (Ramchal) explains that God is the essence of all good. It follows from this that God, who is all good, cannot be together with bad. That is why the Torah states repeatedly that Hashem distances Himself from sinners.

The gift of Yom Kippur is that even though we are sinners Hashem comes close to us. By the very nature of this world, since God cannot be together with bad, one's sins are simply removed. On the day Hashem comes close to us, the day itself becomes our means of atonement.

אי זו היא תשובה גמורה. זה שבא לידו דבר
שעבר בו ואפשר בידו לעשותו ופירש ולא עשה מפני
התשובה. לא מיראה ולא מכשלון כח. כיצד הרי שבא
על אשה בעבירה ולאחר זמן נתייחד עמה והוא עומד
באהבתו בה ובכח גופו ובמדינה שעבר בה ופירש ולא
עבר זהו בעל תשובה גמורה. הוא ששלמה אמר וזכור את
בוראיך בימי בחורותיך. ואם לא שב אלא בימי זקנותו
ובעת שאי אפשר לו לעשות מה שהיה עושה אף על פי
שאינה תשובה מעולה מועלת היא לו ובעל תשובה הוא.
אפילו עבר כל ימיו ועשה תשובה ביום מיתתו ומת
בתשובתו כל עונותיו נמחלין שנאמר עד אשר לא תחשך
השמש והאור והירח והכוכבים ושבו העבים אחר הגשם
שהוא יום המיתה. מכלל שאם זכר בוראו ושב קודם
שימות נסלח לו. ומה היא התשובה הוא שיעזוב
החוטא חטאו ויסירו ממחשבתו ויגמור בלבו שלא
יעשהו עוד שנאמר יעזוב רשע דרכו וגו'. וכן יתנחם
על שעבר שנאמר כי אחרי שובי נחמתי. ויעיד
עליו יודע תעלומות שלא ישוב לזה החטא לעולם
שנאמר ולא נאמר עוד אלקינו למעשה ידינו וגו'.
וצריך להתודות בשפתיו ולומר עניינות אלו שגמר
בלבו.

What is complete repentance? When the thing he had transgressed with comes back to him and he again has the opportunity to do it, and he refrains and does not do so because of the repentance, not because of fear and not because of weakness. For example, one who

sinned with a woman and after some time has passed is
alone with her, and his love for her has endured, and his
bodily strength has remained, and he is in the same place,
and he withdraws and does not transgress—this is a perfect penitent. Of this Shlomo [Hamelech] said: "Remember your Creator in the days of your youth." If he does not
repent until his old age, at the time when it is impossible
to do what he had done, although it is not the most
meritorious penitence, it is meritorious for him and he is
considered a penitent. Even if he transgressed all his life
and repented on the day of his death, and he died penitent,
all his sins are forgiven, as it says, "Before the sun, or the
light, or the moon, or the stars are darkened, and the
clouds return after the rain"—which is an allusion to the
day of death. If he remembered his Creator and repented
before he died, he will be forgiven.

What is repentance? The sinner abandons his sin, and
removes it from his thoughts, and resolves within his heart
not to do it again, as it says, "The wicked shall abandon his
way..." And he will regret that he transgressed, as it says,
"For after I returned, I regretted." And He Who knows all
secrets shall testify that he will not return to the sin forever,
as it says, "We shall not say to the works of our hands—
you are our gods..." He must confess orally and say these
things that he resolved within his heart.

(Rambam, *Hilchos Teshuvah* 2:1-2)

One can raise several questions on these two halachos of
the Rambam. First, why does the Rambam maintain that
perfect *teshuvah* can be achieved only when one finds himself
in the same situation, under the same circumstances, and
decides not to violate that same sin? Doesn't God know a
person's inner intentions and strengths? If a person sincerely
repents in his heart, doesn't Hashem know that his repentance is strong enough to hold him back from violating the
same sin if he were in the same exact situation? Second, what
is the difference between the "perfect" penitent and the *baal
teshuvah* who did not repent until old age or until his deathbed,
if all have their sins forgotten?

Every sin has two aspects to it—the wrongdoing itself
and the damage to creation that the sin brought about. One's
sincere repentance will eliminate his personal sin, but only a
complete reversal of the sin can undo the damage to creation
he made by sinning. If he finds himself actually in the same
situation under the same conditions, and this time controls
himself and does not sin, he is a perfect *baal teshuvah*. The
one who repents in his heart will also have all his sins forgiven, but his repentance cannot be termed "perfect."

There is a third question to be asked on the Rambam:
How can the Rambam state that Hashem will testify that the
baal teshuvah will never return to his sin again? Have we not
seen people repenting and then returning to their sins?

There are two levels of *teshuvah*. One can sincerely repent, and one can become so much in control of his *yetzer
hara* that he actually destroys his inclination for that particular sin. One who has eaten pork throughout his life may
repent, yet at first feels strongly tempted by it. Eventually,
though, he may overcome this temptation and completely
destroy his *yetzer* for it.

To reach the level of destroying one's inclination, one
actually has to go through the experience of controlling
himself while in the same situation. One who sincerely repents in his heart will have his sins forgiven, but he will not
have broken his *yetzer hara*. Only for the one who has destroyed his *yetzer hara*, says the Rambam, will Hashem testify
that he will never return to his sin.

ואל ידמה אדם בעל תשובה שהוא מרוחק ממעלת
הצדיקים מפני העוונות והחטאות שעשה. אין הדבר כן
אלא אהוב ונחמד הוא לפני הבורא כאילו לא חטא
מעולם. ולא עוד אלא ששכרו הרבה שהרי טעם טעם
החטא ופירש ממנו וכבש יצרו. אמרו חכמים מקום
שבעלי תשובה עומדין אין צדיקים גמורין יכולין
לעמוד בו. כלומר מעלתן גדולה ממעלת אלו שלא חטאו
מעולם מפני שהן כובשים יצרם יותר מהם.

> Let not a penitent imagine he is distanced from the heights
> of a righteous man because of his sins and transgressions. It
> is not so; rather, he is as beloved and precious to his Creator
> as if he had never sinned. Not only this, but his reward is
> great, for, after all, he tasted the taste of sin and left it and
> controlled his desire. The Sages have said: In the place that
> penitents stand perfect tzaddikim cannot stand. This is to
> say, the heights they reach are greater than the heights of
> those who never sinned, because they [penitents] conquer
> their desires more than they [who never sinned].
>
> (Rambam, *Hilchos Teshuvah* 7:4)

Now the greatness of a *baal teshuvah* becomes clear. The
perfect *baal teshuvah* has destroyed his *yetzer hara*: Not only has
he left his sin, he has conquered his desire utterly. The Rambam
refers to this by his repetitive language: he "left it and controlled
his desire."

This explains the Rambam's statement (chapter 2, halachah 4) that a *baal teshuvah* should declare that he is a
different person. Now he truly is different, for the perfect
baal teshuvah has destroyed his evil inclination.

✻   ✻   ✻

מדרכי התשובה להיות השב צועק תמיד לפני השם בבכי
ובתחנונים ועושה צדקה כפי כחו.

> It is the way of repentance that the penitent always
> screams before God, in cries and lamentation, and exer-
> cises charity to the utmost of his power...
>
> (Rambam, *Hilchos Teshuvah* 2:4)

Why is the mitzvah of *tzedakah* singled out in the process
of repentance? When one gives away his own money he thus
recognizes that it is not really his. God is the true owner of
everything. Recognizing Hashem and His mastery over all is
the essence of *teshuvah*. Further, the act of giving charity may
be viewed as a means of redeeming oneself from one's sins.

*   *   *

אין התשובה ולא יום הכפורים מכפרין אלא על עבירות
שבין אדם למקום כגון מי שאכל דבר אסור או בעל
בעילה אסורה וכיוצא בהן. אבל עבירות שבין אדם לחבירו
כגון החובל את חבירו או המקלל חבירו או גוזלו
וכיוצא בהן אינו נמחל לו לעולם עד שיתן לחבירו
מה שהוא חייב לו וירצהו. אע"פ שהחזיר לו ממון
שהוא חייב לו צריך לרצותו ולשאול ממנו שימחול לו.
אפילו לא הקניט את חבירו אלא בדברים צריך לפייסו
ולפגע בו עד שימחול לו. לא רצה חבירו למחול לו
מביא לו שורה של שלשה בני אדם מריעיו ופוגעין בו
ומבקשין ממנו. לא נתרצה להן מביא לו שניה ושלישית לא
רצה מניחו והולך לו וזה שלא מחל הוא החוטא. ואם
היה רבו הולך ובא אפילו אלף פעמים עד שימחול לו.

Repentance and Yom Kippur only atone for the sins between man and God; for example, one who ate something
forbidden or had a forbidden relationship and the like.
But sins between man and his fellow man, such as wound-
ing another man, or cursing, or stealing from him, etc., are
not forgiven until he has returned what he is obligated to
give and has pacified him. Even though he returned whatever
money he owed him, he must still pacify him and ask his
forgiveness. Even if he merely taunted him with words, he
must appease him and beg him until he forgives him. If his
fellow does not want to forgive him, he brings a line of three
of his friends and he asks his pardon [in front of them]. If he
is not pacified, he brings them a second and then a third
time. If he [the injured party] still refuses, he leaves and
goes from him, and he who would not forgive is the sinner.
And if it was his teacher he must go to him even a thousand
times until he forgives him.

(Rambam, *Hilchos Teshuvah* 2:9)

Why must a man ask forgiveness from his fellow man in
front of three people? And why need he ask no more than three
times?

אסור לאדם להיות אכזרי ולא יתפייס אלא יהא נוח
לרצות וקשה לכעוס ובשעה שמבקש ממנו החוטא
למחול מוחל בלב שלם ובנפש חפיצה. ואפילו הצר
לו וחטא לו הרבה לא יקום ולא יטור וזהו
דרכם של זרע ישראל ולבם הנכון אבל העובדי
כוכבים ערלי לב אינו כן אלא ועברתן שמרה נצח.
וכן הוא אומר על הגבעונים לפי שלא מחלו ולא
נתפייסו והגבעונים לא מבני ישראל המה.

It is forbidden for a man to be cruel and not appeased;
rather, he should be easily pacified and difficult to anger.
When the sinner asks him to forgive, let him forgive
wholeheartedly and with a willing soul. And even if he
troubled him and sinned greatly against him, let him
not take revenge. This is the way of the seed of Yisrael
and their willing hearts, but the hard-hearted pagans
are not so; the sins against them are perpetually remembered. So it says of the Givonites: Because they would
not forgive and would not be appeased, the Givonim
were not of *Bnei Yisrael*.

(Rambam, *Hilchos Teshuvah* 2:10)

When a person withholds forgiveness in front of three people,
it is a public act, as something done in front of three people will
become known (*Gittin* 33a). By publicly refusing to forgive, he
has committed an act of hard-heartedness, and by repeating this
act three times, the man has created a *chazakah* (legal presump-
tion), and is now classified as a cruel, hard-hearted man. Such a
man, says the Rambam, is considered "not of *Bnei Yisrael*," and
therefore one need not petition for forgiveness.

...הבינונים אם היה בכלל מחצה עונות שלהן שלא הניח
תפילין מעולם דנין אותו כפי חטאו ויש לו חלק
לעולם הבא.

...If among the sins of [one of] the *beinonim* [those with
an equal number of sins and merits] there is included

the sin of never having put on tefillin, he is judged only
by his sins, and he has a portion in the World to Come.
(Rambam, *Hilchos Teshuvah* 3:5)

Tefillin is the Jew's symbol of identification as a Jew. Here
the Rambam emphasizes that even if a Jew separates himself
and doesn't identify himself as a Jew, he still has a portion in
the World to Come.

Shofar and Asmachta

והעברת שופר תרועה בחדש השביעי בעשור לחדש
ביום הכפרים תעבירו שופר בכל ארצכם.

*You shall cause the shofar to sound in the seventh month, on
the tenth day of the month, on the Day of Atonement shall
you sound the shofar in all your land.*
(Vayikra 25:9)

ממשמע שנאמר ביום הכפורים איני יודע שהוא בעשור
לחדש א"כ למה נאמר בעשור לחדש אלא לומר לך
תקיעת עשור לחדש דוחה שבת בכל ארצכם ואין תקיעת
ר"ה דוחה שבת בכל ארצכם אלא בבית דין בלבד.
(רש"י ד"ה ביום הכפורים)

From the words "on the Day of Atonement" do I not
[already] know that it is the tenth of the month? If so,
for what reason does it say "on the tenth day of the
month"? To tell you that the blowing on the tenth of
the month supersedes Shabbos throughout your land,
while the blowing of Rosh Hashanah does not super-
sede Shabbos throughout your land, but only within
the *Beis Din.*
(Rashi ad loc.)

Both the Malbim and the Mizrachi raise a question on Rashi's
words. If the prohibition of blowing a shofar on Shabbos is a rabbini-
cal one, how can it be alluded to in the verse itself? Would it not

then be considered a Torah commandment (*d'oraisa*)?

To better understand Rashi's comment, we must examine the concept of *asmachta*. The Malbim and Mizrachi view an *asmachta* as merely a Biblical allusion to a rabbinic decree; that is, the Rabbonim, upon issuing a law, then refer to the Torah in an attempt to find some hint of it there.

This understanding of the concept, though, doesn't explain Rashi's contention that the words "the tenth of the month" allude to a rabbinic decree.

According to the Ritva (*Rosh Hashanah* 16a), an *asmachta* refers to words actually placed into the text of Torah for the use of Rabbonim. The Torah approved of such a decree; however, it left it up to them whether or not to enact it as a law. The *asmachta* is a halachah of the Rabbonim enacted with the consent of the Torah. With this understanding, the meaning of Rashi's words become clear.

Chanukah

Al Hanissim

על הנסים ועל הפרקן ועל הגבורות ועל התשועות ועל
המלחמות...וזדים ביד עוסקי תורתך.

For the miracles, and for the redemption, and for the
might, and for the salvation, and for the battles...You
delivered evildoers into the hands of those occupied
with Your Torah.

The order of the phrases in *Al Hanissim* is difficult to
understand. Should not the actions—the miracles and the
might—be listed first, followed by the results—redemption
and salvation? Further, shouldn't the "might" be followed by
the greater act—the "miracles"? And why should we mention battle—not victory in battle, but battle itself—as something to be thankful for? Why is Torah singled out; what is its
connection with Chanukah? And, finally, why is the miracle
of the jug of oil not mentioned at all?

The prayer begins with the essential miracle of Chanukah—
for the miracles and for the redemption. A miracle is not a freak

occurrence, it is part of God's plan for the world's redemption. The true miracle of Chanukah was the Jew's recognition of this insight, and thus no mention need be made of the lesser miracle of the jug.

The miracle went even further—for the might and for the salvation. The Jews realized that might, that nature itself, is part of God's plan. The realization of the "might" is actually greater than the understanding of the "miracles" and thus follows it in the listing.

We come to these realizations when we feel our own helplessness and God's might. "There are no atheists in foxholes"—thus we mention the wars that lead us to understanding. Similarly, the study of Torah leads us to this knowledge of God's power and His plan. The Gemara states: "A sign to haughtiness is poverty...What is poverty? Poverty in Torah" (*Kiddushin* 49b). When faced with the infinite wisdom of Torah, one becomes humble. The Torah that brings about humility enabled the Jews to recognize God's hand.

Bearing these ideas in mind, I think one can answer a well-known question brought up about the search for the pure oil. The rule of halachah is that impurity is permitted for public use. For community needs, impurity does not stand in the way; they may use impure oil. If so, why the search?

The philosophical concept behind the principle that impurity is permitted for public use is that the community is so important that impurity does not stand in its way. Yet *Klal Yisrael* had just come to the recognition of their own limitations, and had just achieved a new level of humility. They would not rely on a principle rooted in their own importance!

Hallel

The Taz discusses why *Hallel* is recited on Chanukah, but no *seudah* is eaten, while on Purim the opposite holds true: a *seudah* is eaten, and *Hallel* is not said:

ונראה הטעם דלא קבעו כאן לשמחה כמו בפורים דבפורים
היה הנס מפורסם להצלת נפשות וע"ז יש שמחה בעוה"ז
משא"כ בחנוכה דאע"ג דהיתה ישועה ממנו יתברך במלחמה
מ"מ לא היה מפורסם ע"צ הנס רק בנרות היה הנס מפורסם
ע"כ קבעו להלל ולהודות כי אין מזה שמחה בעוה"ז
והצלת נפשות היה טפל בזה ע"כ עשו עיקר מן הנס
המפורסם שהוא מורה על הודיה כי כן רצונו יתברך
בזה...

It appears that the reason [Chanukah] was not established as a day of joy as in the case of Purim was because
Purim was an obvious miracle of physical salvation. For
this, one rejoices in this world. This is not the case of
Chanukah. Though God did bring salvation through the
war, nevertheless this was not clearly recognized as a miracle;
the open miracle occurred only in the lights. Therefore
they established it [as a day of] praise and thanks, for this
was not merely a time of joy in this world. The physical
salvation was of lesser importance; the essence of the
miracle teaches us to show gratitude...

(*Orach Chayim* 670:2, Taz ad loc.)

The Taz explains that because the Purim miracle in-
volved physical salvation, we mark it with festive celebration. The spiritual miracle of Chanukah embodied in the
discovery of the jug of oil is celebrated through *Hallel*.

The Gemara (*Megillah* 14a), however, does not appear to
give this reason. The Gemara cites three opinions for not
saying *Hallel* on Purim. R. Yitzchak says that one doesn't say
Hallel on a miracle occurring outside of Eretz Yisrael. We do
say it on Pesach, because prior to the Jews' entrance into
Eretz Yisrael, we said *Hallel* on all miracles. This rule came
into effect only after the entrance. R. Nachman explains
that the reading of the Megillah takes the place of *Hallel*,
implying that *Hallel* can be said on a miracle taking place
outside of Eretz Yisrael. Rava says *Hallel* is not recited because its
wording is inappropriate for Purim. The prayer states, "Give
praise, servants of God," but, in fact, even after the Purim

miracle we remained Achashveirosh's subjects. This view,
like that of R. Nachman's, implies that Hallel may be recited
on miracles taking place outside of Eretz Yisrael. None of the
arguments however, seem to take the stand of the Taz.

The question can be explained in the following manner.
As the Taz explains, one says Hallel on a spiritual miracle. R.
Yitzchak holds that all the miracles that were performed for
Am Yisrael on their way to and in Eretz Yisrael are considered
spiritual ones, for they brought about the sanctity of Eretz
Yisrael, as evidenced by the fact that the mitzvah of challah
came into effect only when they entered Eretz Yisrael, while
the mitzvos of bikurim, ma'aser, and terumos began after the
land was settled. Miracles that take place in Eretz Yisrael
since its settlement are also considered spiritual ones, for
they are happening in a holy place.

The argument between R. Yitzchak on one side and R.
Nachman and Rava on the other centers on the question of
whether the miracles that occur today are stepping-stones
towards bringing us back into Eretz Yisrael. If a miracle is
indeed considered a step towards that goal it is a spiritual
miracle, for it will help bring back the sanctity of the land,
when, for example, the mitzvah of yovel will be reestablished.

We see, then, that the Gemara is actually consistent
with the Taz—Hallel is recited only on a miracle of spirituality. Like R. Yitzchak, the Taz appears to feel that a miracle
outside of Eretz Yisrael is not a spiritual one, and therefore
Hallel is not said.

Purim

ויוצא משה את העם לקראת האלקים מן המחנה
ויתיצבו בתחתית ההר.

*Moshe took the people out of the camp to meet God, and
they stood at the foot of the mountain.*

(Shemos 19:17)

...ומדרשו שנתלש ההר ממקומו ונכפה עליהם כגיגית.
(רש"י ד"ה בתחתית ההר)

...The Midrash says: the mountain was taken from its
place and held over them like a barrel.

(Rashi, ad loc.)

ויתיצבו בתחתית ההר אמר ר' אבדימי בר חמא בר
חסא מלמד שכפה הקב"ה עליהם את ההר כגיגית
ואמר להם אם אתם מקבלים התורה מוטב ואם
לאו שם תהא קבורתכם אמר ר' אחא בר יעקב
מכאן מודעא רבה לאורייתא אמר רבא אעפ"כ הדור
קבלוה בימי אחשורוש דכתיב קימו וקבלו היהודים קיימו
מה שקיבלו כבר.

They stood at the foot of the mountain: R. Avdimi son
of Chama son of Chasa said, "This teaches that the
Holy One, blessed be He, held the mountain over them

like a barrel and said to them, 'If you accept the Torah, good; and if not, your burial place will be there.' " R. Acha bar Yaakov said, "This gives a strong excuse against Torah." Rava said, "Nevertheless, they accepted it a second time in the days of Achashveirosh, as it says, 'The Jews fulfilled and accepted'—fulfilled that which they had previously accepted."

(Shabbos 88a)

Chazal explain that at the time of matan Torah, Mt. Sinai was placed above Klal Yisrael. God then gave them a choice: accept the Torah or be buried beneath the mountain. R. Acha maintains: If so, Klal Yisrael has an excuse for not keeping the Torah, for they were forced to accept all the commandments. Answers Rava: Nevertheless, later, in the days of King Achashveirosh, Klal Yisrael voluntarily accepted the Torah.

The Baalei Tosafos raise the question: Why do the Sages claim the Torah was forced on the Jews, when they had previously accepted the Torah of their own volition, with their statement of na'aseh venishma—we will do and we will hear—as it says:

ויענו כל העם יחדו ויאמרו כל אשר דבר ד' נעשה
וישב משה את דברי העם אל ד'.

And the entire nation answered together, and they said: "All that God spoke we will do," and Moshe returned the people's words to God.

(Shemos 19:8)

The Baalei Tosafos respond that God, afraid they would retract their acceptance when faced with the tremendous fires at matan Torah, placed the mountain above them.

This response raises an obvious difficulty: How can Am Yisrael retract their acceptance of the Torah; can we, then, retract that acceptance today?

ועל דא תברתהון אמאי לא קבלתוה אלא כך אומרים
לפניו רבש"ע כלום כפית עלינו הר כגיגית ולא
קבלנוה כמו שעשית לישראל דכתיב ויתיצבו בתחתית
ההר ואמר רב דימי בר חמא מלמד שכפה הקב"ה
הר כגיגית על ישראל ואמר להם אם אתם מקבלין
את התורה מוטב ואם לאו שם תהא קבורתכם מיד
אומר להם הקב"ה הראשונות ישמיעונו שנא'
וראשונות ישמיענו שבע מצות שקיבלתם היכן קיימתם.

And on this [the non-Jewish nations] will be questioned: Why didn't you accept [the Torah]? But so
they will say before Him: Master of the World, did you
hold the mountain over us like a barrel, as you did with
Yisrael, and we didn't accept it? As it says, "They stood
at the bottom of the mountain." And R. Dimi bar Chama
said: This teaches us that the Holy One, blessed be He,
held the mountain over Yisrael like a barrel and said to
them: If you accept the Torah, good; and if not, there
will be your grave.

Immediately the Holy One, blessed be He, will say to
them: Those first [Noachide laws] will testify for us, as
it says, "And announce to us former things" [Yeshay-
ahu 43:9]. The seven mitzvos that you received, how
did you keep them?

(*Avodah Zarah* 2b)

When God will sit in judgment against the other nations,
He will ask why they did not accept the Torah as *Am Yisrael*
did. The other nations will respond that the Jews accepted
only because it was forced upon them, and had God done the
same to them they also would have accepted it. Finally, the
Gemara concludes that the only claim God has against the
other nations is for not observing the seven Noachide laws.
Again, it appears from this Gemara that for some reason the
acceptance of *Klal Yisrael* with their statement of *na'aseh
venishma* was not sufficient, that God had to force their acceptance by holding the mountain over their heads.

Further, if the Torah was accepted voluntarily only during
Achashveirosh's time, does that mean any Jew who violated

the Torah prior to this time was not held responsible for his
wrongdoing?

The Sifri says the following:

ויאמר ד' מסיני בא וגו' (דברים לג:ב) כשנגלה
המקום ליתן תורה לישראל לא על ישראל בלבד הוא
נגלה אלא על כל האומות בתחילה הלך אצל בני
עשו ואמר להם מקבלים אתם את התורה? אמרו לו:
מה כתוב בה? אמר להם: לא תרצח. אמרו לפניו:
רבונו של עולם, כל עצמו של אותו אביהם רוצח
הוא (והידים ידי עשו, בראשית כז:כב) ולא הבטיחו אביו
אלא על החרב (ועל חרבך תחיה, שם שם:מ) אין אנו
יכולים לקבל את התורה. הלך לו אצל בני עמון
ומואב ואמר להם: מקבלים אתם את התורה? אמרו לו:
מה כתוב בה? אמר להם: לא תנאף. אמרו לפניו:
רבונו של עולם, כל עצמם של אותם האנשים אינם
באים אלא מניאוף (ותהרין שתי בנות לוט מאביהן וגו', שם
יט:לו) אין אנו יכולים לקבל את התורה. הלך לו אצל
בני ישמעאל אמר להם: מקבלים אתם את התורה?
אמרו לו: מה כתוב בה? אמר להם: לא תגנוב.
אמרו לפניו: רבונו של עולם, כל עצמם של אותם
האנשים אינם חיים אלא מן הגניבה ומן הגזל
(פרא אדם ידו בכל ויד כל בו, שם טז:יב) אין
אנו יכולים לקבל את התורה. לא היתה אומה
באומות שלא הלך ודיבר ודפק על פתחה אם ירצו
ויקבלו את התורה. ואחר כך בא לו אצל ישראל
אמרו לו: נעשה ונשמע! זהו שנאמר: ד' מסיני בא
וזרח משעיר למו הופיע מהר פארן ואתה מרבבות
קדש מימינו אש דת למו.

And he said: "The Lord came from Sinai," etc. (Devarim
33:2). When the Divine Presence revealed Himself to
give the Torah to Yisrael, He did not reveal Himself
only to Yisrael, but, rather, to all the nations. At first
He went to the sons of Esav and said to them: "Will you
accept the Torah?" They said to Him: "What is written
within?" He said to them: "Do not kill." They responded:
"Master of the World, the entire existence of our father
is to be a killer ('The hands are the hands of Esav'—
Bereishis 27:22), and his father [Yitzchak] promised
him nothing but the sword ('By your sword you shall

live'—Bereishis 27:40). We cannot accept the Torah."

He went to the sons of Ammon and Moav and said to them: "Will you accept the Torah?" They said to Him: "What is written within?" He said to them: "You shall not commit adultery." They responded: "Master of the World, our entire existence comes only from adultery ('The two daughters of Lot became pregnant from their father'— Bereishis 19:36). We cannot accept the Torah."

He went to the sons of Yishmael. He said to them: "Will you accept the Torah?" They said: "What is written within?" He said to them: "Do not steal." They responded: "Master of the World, our entire existence is only to live by stealing and robbery ('He will be a wild man, his hand will be against every man, and every man's hand against him'—Bereishis 16:12). We cannot accept the Torah."

There was no nation among the nations that He did not approach and speak with and knock upon their door to ask if they wished to receive the Torah. And afterwards He went to Yisrael, and they said: "We will do and we will hear!" as is written: "The Lord came from Sinai, and rose up from Seir to them, He appeared from Mt. Paran, and He came from holy multitudes—from His right hand a fiery law went out to them" (Devarim 33:2).

(Sifri, Devarim 33:2)

When God offered the Torah to the other nations, each inquired about its contents and each found a different commandment he could not possibly observe. Then God presented the Torah to *Bnei Yisrael*, who responded with *na'aseh venishma*.

It showed tremendous greatness on the part of the Jews to accept the Torah without inquiring about its contents. However, such an acceptance also has its limitations. It is an acceptance of blind faith rather than one based on a real appreciation of the Torah's contents, of the mitzvos.

Later, as the Gemara shows, the other nations complained that when *Am Yisrael* accepted the Torah it was done without the knowledge of its demands. When faced with these demands, they accepted it only because God had placed a mountain over them. Had this been done to us, claimed the other nations, we, too, would have accepted the Torah.

Let us analyze the difference between accepting the Torah without knowledge of what it contains (the acceptance of *na'aseh venishma*) and the acceptance that came later with the knowledge of its mitzvos. When one accepts the Torah without ascertaining its contents first, one is saying he will subjugate himself to whatever God demands of him. If one accepts the Torah with the full awareness of its mitzvos, one makes a greater statement: He says the mitzvos themselves have intrinsic value and significance.

The practical difference between these two commitments is the issue of doing beyond what the Torah demands, of glorifying the mitzvos. One who accepted only subjugation to God's Will will do whatever God demands of him. Since he never accepted that the mitzvos themselves have significance, he will not glorify the mitzvos beyond his simple obligation. However, one who accepts the Torah with the knowledge of its mitzvos and their inherent significance will fulfill them in the most perfect fashion.

The Gemara recognizes that when Yisrael said the words *na'aseh venishma*, they became responsible for their wrongdoing. If so, what is the "excuse against the Torah" and the performance of mitzvos? Because *Bnei Yisrael* accepted the Torah without knowledge of its mitzvos, they never made a statement showing that they appreciated their value, and therefore had no reason to do beyond the minimum. Asks the Gemara: Does *Am Yisrael* now have an excuse not to glorify any of the mitzvos? The Gemara answers that there was a second acceptance of the Torah during the time of Achashveirosh; this was the acceptance that the mitzvos themselves have significance.

Pesach:
The Hagaddah

Ha Lachma Anya

השתא הכא לשנה הבאה בארעא דישראל. השתא
עבדי לשנה הבאה בני חורין.

This year we are here, next year in Eretz Yisrael; this
year we are slaves, next year we will be free.

Why is the entering into Eretz Yisrael mentioned before
becoming free? Isn't freedom the prerequisite for entrance
into Eretz Yisrael?

Real freedom is involvement in Torah, as our Sages have
said: "No man is free unless he busies himself with Torah."

As pointed out in *Parshas Bereishis*, the total fulfillment
of Torah can be achieved only in Eretz Yisrael. Therefore, in
order to achieve real freedom, the freedom of Torah, one
must first come to Eretz Yisrael.

*   *   *

הא לחמא עניא די אכלו אבהתנא בארעא דמצרים.
כל דכפין ייתי ויכול כל דצריך ייתי ויפסח.

This is the bread of affliction that our ancestors ate in
Egypt. All who are hungry come and eat; all who are in
need come and partake of the Pesach.

If this is truly an invitation to the poor, why do we invite
them only after we have already said *Kiddush?* And why do
we mention the matzah and then issue our invitation?

Pesach represents the celebration of our freedom. A free
man, however, often loses his sensitivity to others. A person who
suffers can more easily feel compassion for one in a similar situation. Once a person is free, he may forget and lose that sensitivity.

This declaration, "All who are hungry can come and
eat," is not an actual invitation. A true invitation would have
been given before even sitting down to the Seder.

The words reflect the emotions that one should feel this
day: Although we are celebrating freedom we must not lose
our sensitivity to others. We refer to the matzah, symbol of
our freedom, and then, immediately, show concern for the
needy and destitute among us.

Mah Nishtanah

Why is the command "You will tell your son that day"
(Shemos 13:8) stated in reference to Pesach? Why is it only
on Pesach that a child questions us about the Yom Tov?

Pesach is the celebration of freedom. Actually, there are
many free men who work harder than slaves. The difference
between a slave and a free man is that a free man feels in
control of his destiny and thus cares about his future. The
ultimate symbol of any human being's future is his children.
Therefore on Pesach, when we celebrate freedom, we show

we are free by educating our children. We demonstrate this by having them ask the questions about the holiday.

The Four Sons

חכם מה הוא אומר. מה העדות והחקים והמשפטים אשר צוה ד' אלקינו אתכם. ואף אתה אמר לו כהלכות הפסח. אין מפטירין אחר הפסח אפיקומן.

What does the wise one say? What are the testimonies, and the statutes, and the laws which the Lord, our God, has commanded you? You, in turn, instruct him as in the laws of Pesach: One takes no dessert (*afikoman*) after the Pesach.

רשע מה הוא אומר. מה העבודה הזאת לכם. לכם ולא לו ולפי שהוציא את עצמו מן הכלל כפר בעקר ואף אתה הקהה את שניו.

What does the wicked one say? What is this service to you? "To you" and not to himself! Because he excluded himself from the community, he denied the fundamental. Therefore you should blunt his teeth....

When the wise son excludes himself from the mitzvos with the words "commanded you," why do we not rebuke him as we do the wicked son for his words "to you"? And how does our reply to the wise son, "one takes no dessert after the Pesach," answer his question?

The wise son wonders what the mitzvos achieve for a person. He does not refuse to perform them; he is disturbed by their philosophical underpinnings. We tell him that just as one may not eat after the *Karban Pesach* so that he doesn't lose the taste and effect of the *Karban*, so he must understand that all the mitzvos have an effect on every Jew who performs them, whether or not they understand the reasoning behind them. Questions on the philosophy of the mitzvos do not exclude the wise son from performing them; thus, no rebuke is given.

The wicked son, however, questioned not the underlying philosophy of the mitzvos; he referred to the actions themselves. "What is this service to you?" he asks, as if to poke fun at it. To such a person we respond by "blunting his teeth."

Shavuos

Shabbos and Shavuos are similar in several ways. Shabbos represents the culmination of seven days, Shavuos the culmination of seven weeks. Both have no mitzvos from the Torah that mandate specific bodily action. Though one must make *Kiddush* on Shabbos, only the actual recitation of the words comes from the Torah, while making *Kiddush* on wine is rabbinic in origin. On Shavuos *Kiddush* is a rabbinic decree.

Why do neither Shabbos nor Shavuos have the obligation of physical action? One must first understand the difference between a mitzvah expressed through action and one not so fulfilled. Anything expressed through the physical by definition has a limitation to it. In addition, when a mitzvah has a physical action attached to it, it may inspire performance of the mitzvah by those who lack belief in its ideology: How many unbelieving Jews observe Pesach because of the beauty of the Seder? Third, when a mitzvah has a physical manifestation, even those who believe in its underlying philosophy tend to perform it out of rote, often neglecting the philosophy of the mitzvah during its performance.

Shabbos and Shavuos are the two most fundamental days of the Jewish religion. The observance of Shabbos testifies to one's belief that God created the world; the observance of Shavuos testifies to one's belief that He gave the Torah. The Torah wanted that the observance of such fundamental days be performed wholly through our conscious belief in their ideology, without the limitations of the physical; they should not be observed for their beauty, nor performed dully and without thought.

WORDS OF SILENCE

Words of Silence

*The following was presented during the shloshim
at the Riverdale Jewish Center.*

My father, may he live to one hundred and twenty, asked me to speak today to represent both of us. This morning and throughout the *shiva* I have heard many things about my mother, some that I knew and some perhaps that I didn't know. She always knew what to say, she always had a compliment, she always had a smile, she always sensed what had to be done in community work and stood up to the occasion. But being a son and being so close to my mother, perhaps I can explain what in her personality created such greatness.

Chazal say in *Pirkei Avos* (1:17):

> Shimon, [Rabban Gamliel's] son, says: "My entire life I have grown up among wise men and I never found anything greater than silence..."

A strange statement. So much can be communicated through words, all knowledge is communicated through words, so many of our relationships are created through words—yet the Mishnah says that greater than all of that is silence. How strange. If one looks a little bit closer, and stops for a second and thinks, one sees that the Mishnah is not denying expression, it is telling us a secret: there is an expression beyond the expression of words. There is an expression that is from silence.

What is this expression of silence? There is another Mishnah in *Pirkei Avos* (2:13):

> [Rabban Yochanan ben Zakkai said to his disciples]: "Go out and see what is the proper way to which a man should cling." Rabbi Eliezer says: "A good eye" [one who isn't jealous of his fellow man]. Rabbi Yehoshua says: "A good friend." Rabbi Yose says: "A good neighbor." Rabbi Shimon says: "One who sees the inevitable," [and the Bartenura explains his meaning: "One who is capable of analyzing a situation"]. Rabbi Elazar says: "A good heart." He [Rabban Yochanan ben Zakkai] says to them: "It appears to me that the words of Elazar ben Arach are the proper ones, for everything everyone else has said is included in what he has said."

"A good heart" encompasses everything else. Again, a strange *Chazal*. What does it mean that "a good heart" enables one to analyze the situation?

Having a good heart does not simply mean I am kind, I do people favors. That, perhaps, can be incorporated in being a good friend or good neighbor. Having a good heart has a much deeper meaning. It is referring to the ability to allow one's heart to cling to everyone else's heart. It is referring to the one who can feel other people's feelings, who can sense their sensitivities. It is referring to the one who can feel and understand what another person needs at this very moment—what the individual needs, what the community needs. Only one who allows his heart to feel and sense everyone else's heart can analyze a situation. A good heart is that expression of silence.

It is clear to me now how my mother always knew what

to say and when to say it, how she always knew when to smile, how she always knew what the individual needed and what the community needed. It is regarding an individual like my mother that *Chazal* say a good heart encompasses all. It is regarding an individual like my mother that *Chazal* say nothing is greater than silence, than one who is capable of communicating through silence and allowing her heart to sense and feel everybody else's heart. In my entire life, for all my years of growing up, I never remember my mother yelling at me or hitting me. It wasn't necessary. She was capable of communicating all her thoughts and all her feelings simply by looking into my heart through the words of silence.

It is no secret to anybody here the great marriage my father and mother had, but it wasn't that they sat in the evening in constant discussion. They could be sitting in a room and not a single word would be said. But yet being in that room, you felt expressions and love passing between them: words of silence. Their hearts talked to each other. When that unfortunate tragedy happened in our family and my brother, Dovid *z"l*, was *niftar*, it was my mother who held the family together. But it wasn't through constant discussions; she communicated through silence her strength, her greatness, and through that my father and I were also able to be strong.

How beautiful is that *Chazal*: "Words that go out of one's heart can enter the hearts of others." It is the communication of silence, of allowing one's heart to cling to someone else's heart, that surpasses all communication.

The Rambam in *Hilchos Melachim* describes the definition of a king. He does not define him by his strength or by his power. He gives one simple definition: A king is one whose heart is the heart of the entire Jewish people, the one who is sensitive to everyone else's feelings. My mother was truly such a queen.

I stand before you today and both my father and I have a

lot to thank all of you, as a community, as individuals. We have a lot to thank you for, for your expressions of recent concern. But let me conclude that it is not necessary for us to express our feelings in words. I think the greatest expression that we can give you is the expression of silence. Words that go out of one's heart can enter the hearts of others.

And now I turn to you, Daddy. My heart touches your heart and expresses thoughts of love through silence. I express to you the strength that my mother *z"l* would want us to have. We have a legacy to give over to our children, to all the grandchildren, not only what Mommy represented, but that special personality trait that Mommy had: the ability to look at one's *panim*, face, and see their *p'nim*, their heart. May *Hakadosh Baruch Hu* give you long life so that you can witness the bar mitzvos, the *chasunos*, and all the *simchos* of all your grandchildren. Amen.

Glossary

Akeres Habayis: Mainstay of the home; homemaker.
Am Yisrael: The nation of Israel.
Asmachta: Scriptural hints at a Rabbinically derived law.
Avodah Zarah: Idol worship.
Avos: Patriarchs.

Baal Teshuva: A penitent.
Bayis: House.
Be'er: Well.
Beis Hamikdash: Temple.
Berachos: Blessings.
Bikurim: Offering of the first fruits.
Bnei Yisrael: The children of Israel, i.e., the people of Israel.
Bris: Covenant; circumcision.
Bris Bein Habesarim: God's covenant with Avraham in which he promises him Eretz Yisrael.

Chachamim: Sages.
Challah: The portion taken from dough and given to the Kohanim.
Chazakah: Status quo.
Chazal: The Sages.
Chesed: Lovingkindness.
Chumrah: Stringency.

D'oraisa: From the Torah, i.e., a commandment derived directly from the Torah's words, as opposed to one Rabbinic in nature.

Eretz Yisrael: Land of Israel.

Gaon: Genius.
Gematria: Interpretations based on numerical value of letters and words.

Halachah: Jewish law.
Hashem: God.

Korban: Sacrifice.
Kareis: The punishment of excision.
Klal Yisrael: The community of Israel.
Kohen, Kohanim: Priest, priests.

Ma'aras Hamachpelah: Cave of Machpelah—burial plot of the Patriarchs in Hebron.
Ma'aser: Tithe—one tenth of one's produce given to the Levi'im.
Matan Torah: Giving of the Torah.
Mesorah: Transmission of Jewish tradition.
Midos: Character traits.

Na'aseh Venishma: "We will do and we will hear"—Israel's acceptance of the Torah.
Nazir: One who vows to avoid wine, cut his hair, and avoid being in the presence of a corpse.
Nisuin: Jewish marriage.

Olam Habah: World to Come.
Olam Hazeh: The physical world.
Orlah: Foreskin cut off at circumcision.

Parah Adumah: Red heifer whose ashes were used for ritual purification.
Parshah, Parshas: The weekly Torah portion.
Pasuk: Verse.

Seudah: Festive meal.

Shidduch: Prospective marriage partner.
Shiva: Seven-day mourning period.
Shloshim: Thirty-day mourning period.
Shmittah: Sabbatical year.
Siyata Dishmaya: Heaven's help and guidance.

Taryag Mitzvos: 613 commandments of the Torah.
Terumah: Offering given to the priest.
Teshuvah: Repentance.
Tzedakah: Charity.

Yetzer: Inclination.
Yetzer Hara: Evil inclination.
Yibum: Levirate marriage, i.e., the obligation to marry the widow of a childless brother in order to perpetuate his name.
Yovel: Jubilee year.